THE
APPRENTICE
A-Z

THE
APPRENTICE
A-Z

THE TOTALLY UNOFFICIAL GUIDE
TO THE HIT TV SERIES

CHARLIE
BURDEN

JOHN BLAKE

Published by John Blake Publishing Ltd,
3 Bramber Court, 2 Bramber Road,
London W14 9PB, England

www.johnblakepublishing.co.uk

www.facebook.com/Johnblakepub facebook
twitter.com/johnblakepub twitter

First published in paperback in 2011

ISBN: 9781843583950

British Library Cataloguing-in-Publication Data:

A catalogue record for this book is available from the British Library.

Design by www.envydesign.co.uk

Printed in Great Britain by CPI Bookmarque Ltd, Croydon CR0 4TD

1 3 5 7 9 10 8 6 4 2

Papers used by John Blake Publishing are natural, recyclable products made
from wood grown in sustainable forests. The manufacturing processes
conform to the environmental regulations of the country of origin.

Photographs © Wenn

INTRODUCTION

The Apprentice A-Z is the definitive guide to Britain's best-loved and most-enduring business programme. Here you will find out everything you ever wanted to know about the 'job interview from hell' that has so captured our imagination in recent years. Including behind-the-scenes secrets and marvellous memories, the book is packed with facts about the much-loved BBC institution.

You will discover how the show was first inspired by the sight of ants feeding on a carcass in the Amazonian jungle, find out what happened next to the candidates who won each series and learn the entrepreneurial secrets that jettisoned them to business success. We will also take a look at how the *Apprentice* franchise works elsewhere in the world, from America to Turkey. Discover the shocking off-air rows that led to Lord

Sugar considering quitting the entire project, relive the side-splitting moments of the zanier characters like Stuart Baggs (the brand) and loud mouths such as Katie 'Cruella de Vil' Hopkins.

From Margaret Mountford to scholarships at Sandhurst, from kosher chickens in Morocco to cups of tea at the Bridge End Cafe, all *Apprentice* life is here. Whether you want to reach the top in business, find out what goes on when the cameras are switched off or simply relive some of the finest British television of recent years, this must-have book will inform, delight and entertain you.

A is for...

ALAN SUGAR (aka Lord Sugar, Sir Alan, Suralan, Sir A, Sir Sugar)

Belligerent, blunt and brilliant, Lord Sugar is more than just the public face or star of *The Apprentice*. He is the very personification of the dual themes of the series. Sugar's meteoric rise in the world of business, and estimated personal worth of £800 million, serve as inspirations to budding entrepreneurs. Simultaneously, his fearsome manner and merciless way of communicating remind them of the harsh realities of the industry they aspire to join. Without his unforgiving, clear-eyed and bristling presence, the programme would be an entirely different,

Sir Alan at Viglen. The computing giant's chief executive is an *Apprentice* interviewer.

inferior prospect. He is irreplaceable, as central and crucial to the show's appeal as is Simon Cowell to the *X Factor*.

Before he came to public attention through the show, Sugar had already spent 40 eventful years as a businessman, during which even media magnate Rupert Murdoch had been moved to describe him as 'probably Britain's greatest entrepreneur'. Sugar's journey to the top was inspiring and eventful. Born in 1947 by caesarean section, Alan Michael Sugar was the youngest of four children. With 11 years between him and his nearest sibling, he felt in many ways like an 'only child'. He grew up in Hackney, east London. The capital was recovering from the Second World War and these were tough times in a rough neighbourhood.

From an early age, he began to show the signs of enterprise that would see him rise. For instance, one of his key skills in business has been as a salesman. Even when he was a mere schoolboy, his headmaster took admiring note of the bright pupil's powers of persuasion. At the age of 12, as has become legendary, he was rising at the crack of dawn to boil beetroots for a local greengrocer. Then he launched an amateur photography business, snapping photos of people's families for money. He was a grafter while still in short trousers.

Through keen, hungry eyes, he continued to spot

opportunities to make money and pursued them with energy and courage. By the time he left school, his income was higher than that of his father, a tailor. Indeed, Sugar's parents often viewed his enterprising ways with concern and fear. He was not to be held back. Once free from school he was able to widen his business ventures and he did so with focus and determination. He sold everything from cigarette lighters to car aerials. He launched his own electronics company, Amstrad, in the 1960s. He was just 21 years of age. The company name is inspired by his own name: it is an acronym of Alan Michael Sugar Trading. During the following decade it grew and grew, until in 1980 he floated it on the stock exchange. By this time Amstrad had become a force to be reckoned with in several sectors, including those of hi-fis and personal computers.

Already a success, he thrived and blossomed further during the entrepreneurial atmosphere of the 1980s. It was a decade made for people such as him. 'There's a new breed of person coming up – the likely lad,' said Sugar during the 1980s. 'You see it in the City and everywhere. It's no longer Mr Heathcote-Smythe's son who's getting the job.' There were few likelier lads than he in British business in those times: in 1987 his personal worth was in the region of £600 million. That year's stock-market crash hit his company hard for a while, but Amstrad and Sugar bounced back. The business world had changed for ever and Sugar was all the happier for the changes. 'The establishment was smashed, definitely,' he said. 'The old-school tie went out the window. Anybody can do anything now.'

The man that viewers see on *The Apprentice* is very much the same as the man people back then encountered in everyday business meetings. A business contact who sat in meetings between Sugar and the *Dixons* electronics chain said that they were often feisty summits. 'These were not meetings where you would want to talk unless you had to because you would get ripped apart – by your own side if not the other,' said the source. 'They were fighting over volume and percentage points for hours and hours.' These were every bit as fearsome as the boardroom showdowns of *The Apprentice*. The air would turn blue and desks were thumped. However, once the business of the day was concluded, hands would be shaken and laughter would be shared.

He is an undeniable British success story, but not everything Sugar has touched turned to gold. When he got involved in football in 1991, it turned out to be a rollercoaster ten years. He became the chairman of his favourite team, Tottenham Hotspur, but his

Sugar's old headquarters in Brentwood, Essex, were turned into a hotel.

experience of the beautiful game was bruising. He contributed a huge amount to the club, not least paying off over £20 million of debts to get it back on its feet. But he and Terry Venables endured a tumultuous relationship that ended up with the popular manager being sacked. 'I felt as though I'd killed Bambi,' said Sugar, accurately describing the extent of the wrath he faced from the fans after he told Venables: 'You're fired.'

His football reign also did nothing to give him a positive perception of professional footballer as a class. 'They're scum, total scum,' he said, with typical, to-the-point candour. 'They don't know what honesty or loyalty is. They're the biggest scum that walk on this planet and, if they weren't football players, most of them would be in prison, it's as simple as that.' He and Venables ended up embroiled in a court battle, during which the abuse Sugar faced from angry Spurs fans became all the more bitter and threatening. His family, too, were targeted and Sugar eventually decided to walk away from the game.

He has endured his fair share of high-profile embarrassments. In 2005 he predicted that the iPod would not be a lasting success. 'Next Christmas the iPod will be dead, finished, gone, kaput,' he said. He then watched with surprise as Apple sold hundreds of millions of units of its famous MP3 player. He would

TERRY VENABLES MANAGED TOTTENHAM WHEN LORD SUGAR OWNED THEM.

have liked to have enjoyed a slice of that success when he launched his e-mailer product, a telephone that also allowed the user to send emails. It was launched to great fanfare, with the *Mail On Sunday* claiming it was 'the most important mass market electronic product since he kick-started Britain's personal computer market fifteen years ago'. Instead it proved an embarrassing and costly disaster, and one that is still to this day held against him by critics.

He has successfully branched into other business spheres, including IT, private-jet hire, property and screen advertising. He had appeared on television, on shows such as *The Money Programme*, before he was hired for *The Apprentice* in 2005. He had also gained public recognition during his football years. However, it was *The Apprentice* that truly made him a public face and a famous name. Rarely, though, has a celebrity had so many names. He went from Alan Sugar to Sir Alan and then the cheeky diminutive 'Suralan'. One of the production team that first hired him for the show always referred him to as simply 'Sir A'. No wonder people got confused by these many monikers. 'I do apologise, Sir Sugar,' said Phil Tufnell when he arrived late for a boardroom meeting in *Sport Relief Does The Apprentice*. 'Sir Alan,' replied Sugar sternly.

But is he really as moody and mean as he sometimes

comes across onscreen? 'What you see is me, there's no acting, and the same goes for the apprentices,' he said during the first series run. However, he has since complained that the final cut of the show sometimes presents him as sterner than he really is. His personality is certainly key to the appeal of the series. The *Independent* newspaper accurately described him as 'its honey-trap character, a magnetic personality who emerges during the series and stealthily gets you obsessed'. His putdowns are pithy and memorable, his overall persona threatening and terrifying. When a candidate mourned a lack of fairness, Sugar gave her short shrift. 'Fair? The only fair you're gonna get is your bloody train fare home!' he said. To another candidate, he said: 'You seem to have gone from anchor to wanker.' This is not an arena for the sensitive or meek, as he once told the contestants: 'If you survive here, I promise you this: as sure as I've got a hole in my bloody arse, when it's down to two of you, people that are nice about you *now*...will not be.'

Grumpy? You'd better believe it, but always entertainingly and with compassion. In fact, his no-nonsense way with words, quotable turns of phrase and willingness to play the 'baddie' he shows on *The Apprentice* has been a feature of his career for as long as anyone can remember. In April 1987 he gave a colourful and memorable lecture to business students at a London university, in which he gave a snappy description of what his firm was all about and where it stood in the business field. 'Pan Am takes good care of you,' he said. 'Marks & Spencer loves you. IBM says the customer is king. At Amstrad, we want your money!'

Niceties are usually at a minimum when Lord Sugar talks business, as even the great and the good of the stock market have learned. Asked what his company's P/E (price-to-earnings) ratio is, he replied as if he believed that 'P/E' meant physical education. 'Twenty press-ups every morning,' he said. When asked about a rival company he was suitably damning, describing it as 'like a lost lamb with a shopping basket'. These are not pre-rehearsed lines. His sayings roll off his tongue so naturally and effortlessly, it is as if he was born to be on television. However, he makes for a slightly uncomfortable media celebrity. For years, he was more than unhappy about giving interviews to the media. When he was eventually convinced to face a journalist, he was often tetchy during the chat. 'Is there a Sugar "brand"?' one journalist asked him. 'Yes, Tate & Lyle,' was his off-the-cuff reply.

When it came to the launch of *The Apprentice*, who else in the business world but Sugar could have carried off the role of the no-nonsense boss, ready to tear shreds

PRINCE CHARLES MEETS LORD SUGAR AND HIS WIFE ANN.

off incompetent candidates, put the wind up everyone and then fearsomely point his finger at each week's sacrificial lamb and tell them: 'You're fired'? As one television executive said, if Richard Branson had been chosen, he wouldn't have been able to stop smiling, even as he was firing someone. Sir Phillip Green had been the BBC's first choice for the role, but he was too busy preparing a take-over of Marks & Spencer. Ryanair boss Michael O'Leary was also approached, but turned the offer down. Even the then BBC director general Greg Dyke was considered for a major role on the show.

But Sugar was a good choice, the natural person to turn to. Donald Trump, who anchors the original US version of *The Apprentice*, said he is delighted by Sugar's performances. 'He does a good job over there,' Trump told *Seven* magazine. 'I chose him with [*Apprentice* creator Mark Burnett]. We have tried this format in lots of countries with different entrepreneurs and Alan has done it best.' Sugar was not troubled by the fact he was not first choice for the show. As soon as he was approached he made it clear that he was keen to take part. 'I'm sure they knocked on all the usual suspects' doors before they got to me but, while some businessmen may be clever and bright, they can dry up in front of camera,' he said. 'I really think it opens a window into the business world, and that's why I do it. I know that top businessmen profess to think it's all a bit of a joke but, while they're sitting there calling the candidates a bunch of pricks, they're all glued to the programme.'

A good, balanced insight into Sugar's personality was offered by series-one winner Tim Campbell. He said, 'He's a tough man. Some people say he's a pussycat – he's not. You don't get to where he got by letting people walk over you. You don't see the other side of him on *The Apprentice* though; he's a family man, he can be incredibly funny and he's incredibly generous – he's practically built the Hackney Empire and he's supported Great Ormond Street very well. I've got a lot of respect for him.' So do *The Apprentice* fans, for whom he is the key ingredient of the 'glue' that keeps us all watching. *The Apprentice* would be unimaginable without him. Long may he reign.

DID YOU KNOW?

Lord Sugar is a qualified pilot, who owns an £18.5 million Embraer Legacy 650 private jet and a Legacy 600 jet, worth an estimated £15 million. In 2008 he walked away unhurt after a scary landing in Manchester during a thunderous storm.

Lord Sugar's niece, Rita Simons, appears in the BBC soap opera *Eastenders* as Roxy Mitchell.

He once weighed 14st 7lb, but lost three stone after taking up cycling.

RITA SIMONS – ACTRESS AND NIECE OF LORD SUGAR.

In an absent-minded moment on a busy day in the office, he once signed a birthday card to his wife 'Best wishes, Sir Alan Sugar.'

He has been awarded two honorary Doctorates of Science degrees, in 1988 from City University and in 2005 from Brunel University.

IN 2005 SIR ALAN RECEIVED AN HONORARY DOCTORATE FROM BRUNEL UNIVERSITY.

AUDITIONS

Ever wondered how the *Apprentice* candidates get to be on the show? Around 10,000 people audition every year to take part in the series. The application process begins when they fill in the online form. The most impressive applicants are chosen to attend regional interview/auditions around the country. A flavour of these gatherings was served up by *Mirror* journalist Julie McCaffrey, who submitted herself to one such audition in Glasgow, so she could write about what goes on at them. McCaffrey wrote that she encountered some of the rudest people of her life, adding that at the auditions, 'the air is thick with smugness'. Competitiveness, too. For instance, when one of her fellow applicants was called to be interviewed while he was in the toilet, a rival thought nothing of pretending the temporarily absent applicant had given up and gone home.

When McCaffrey was interviewed by a member of the production team he asked her: 'What makes you think you could handle Sir Alan's dressing-downs?' Other questions included: 'Do you really think you can win?' and 'What's your strategy?' She managed to bluff her way through to the next round of the audition, where she was met with a fierce and fast round of questions. Among those thrown at her during her interrogation were: 'How would you cope if your group was given a deadline you knew was impossible to meet? What do you think of Sir Alan as a boss and a mentor? What's the last groundbreaking thing you did?'

For the third round she faced yet more questions, but this time from a panel. This time she was asked if she had a good sense of humour and then asked to prove it by telling a joke. She did so, but provoked precious little mirth. She was then quizzed on her knowledge of Amstrad and Lord Sugar's career, as well as facing more questions about her own business prowess. Then it was on for the 'screen test', in which she was asked more questions about herself but this time on camera. After returning home, she learned that she was not successful in securing a place on the programme, but at least she kept her journalistic cover long enough to see how the process works. When Richard Tyler attempted to research a similar story for the *Daily Telegraph* he was lambasted by 'an angry young woman' from the production team for his 'intrusion', and marched away from the proceedings in an exit as ignominious as that of any fired *Apprentice* candidate.

After the regional interviews, a shortlist of around 75 applicants is drawn up and the chosen ones are invited to a second round of scrutiny in London. Here, the selection process becomes all the tougher. The candidates are assessed in groups and asked to do various exercises to test their business acumen and to what extent they are team players. During this stage, the egos need to be set aside in favour of a team purpose, which proves a test too far for some. After these rounds the list is cut down to around 20 or 30 applicants. Those are assessed by a psychologist and asked for references, which are carefully checked. There are also checks for any criminal records, though occasionally some such details have been missed (see FRAUD). It is from this group that the final line-up for the programme is chosen.

Lord Sugar is keenly involved in the selection of the candidates for the show. 'I always look at the final CVs and scrutinise every one,' he said. As he later explained, it is important at this stage to filter out contestants who were applying out of a desire for television fame, rather than to learn about business and become the next *Apprentice*. 'It was new to me six years ago and we attracted a certain category but we are very conscious of that now and we want proper business people, although occasionally one slips through the net,' he said.

All the same, it is a difficult balancing act. The candidates do need to be entertaining – and they frequently are from the very start. The audition videos

SERIES FIVE APPRENTICES KATE WALSH AND PHILIP TAYLOR.

of the successful applicants are often released on the internet. The most entertaining of them was that of the legendary Stuart Baggs (the brand), of series six. 'People like me intimidate me,' he said, showing from the off that his lack of self-awareness was not dwarfed by his plentiful self-belief. Explaining how exciting his life to date had been, he said: 'Even when I'm sleeping, I'm not really sleeping.' He then added that he liked to take chances: 'Why not? I'm alive. There are so many people that... aren't alive, or who have died unfortunately. Now, I'm alive – that's a gift frankly.' It is indeed – where would any of us be without life?

Elsewhere, Melissa Cohen reeled off a list of less than ideal names she had been called during her life, including The Battering Ram and The Bulldozer. 'I generally get people quite scared, I don't know why,' she said. Laura Moore described herself as 'ballsy', adding: 'My boss does joke that I'm a man trapped in a woman's body.' Jamie Lester preferred to attempt some clichés, and even struggled with one of those. 'I'm... I'm a big believer that you got... you get, you get what you, er, get... get what you give,' he said. He did better when he said: 'You've gotta break eggs to make an omelette – it's as simple as that.' Meanwhile, Dan Harris said: 'I'm an all-round package – I think I'm going to win this.' As it turned out, he was fired in week one.

Sometimes, the audition videos of some entertaining applicants who did *not* make it to the show have also been released. A number of them were shown struggling answering questions about 'loss leaders' and 'gross profit', some sang and others did the splits or press-ups to try and prove their worth. In one of them a woman described herself as 'a controlled nuclear fusion', adding: 'I don't just transmit energy, I am light itself.' It's a shame she didn't get onto the show itself; she would presumably have been a shining example to all.

B is for...

BIG MOUTHS

Given the competitive, cut-throat nature of the business world and the pressure on contestants to stand out for television viewers, it is little surprise that *The Apprentice* has attracted many noisy and boastful people throughout its reign. As chat-show host Michael Parkinson once observed, many *Apprentice* candidates are: 'Vulgar, loud people, who, for all the wrong reasons, are dobbing each other in.' The old curmudgeon was not far wrong. Here are some of those vulgar people, who will be remembered for ever as the big mouths of *The Apprentice*...

Jo Cameron

Flame-haired Jo arrived at *The Apprentice* well-equipped for the challenge. She was the founding director of a training company, had a diploma in Life Coaching and bags of personality. Full of energy and definitely at the zany end of the business market, she quickly became a stand-out character who people either loved or loathed. She was rarely far from anything exciting or controversial that happened, guaranteeing her plenty of attention and admiration from the viewing public, if not always much of the latter from her fellow contestants.

She survived three boardroom showdowns before she was finally fired after her fourth time on a losing team. During one of the boardroom sessions she was told by Sugar: 'I don't know if you're just a bloody nutter!' It was one of the series' more memorable quotations. However, he so admired the doughty defence she put up for herself that he put aside his 'nutter' fears and let her stay another week. Finally, in week six, her time was up. After a terrible performance from her in the car-selling task, Sugar finally told her she was fired. Even then, she was not to be silenced. She tried repeatedly to argue with his decision but he kept repeating it until she gave up.

In the aftermath of her *Apprentice* experience Cameron has put her big mouth to good use by

PRESENTER SARAH CAWOOD WITH *APPRENTICE* CONTESTANT
MICHELLE DEWBERRY.

becoming a motivational speaker and winning an *Apprentice*-themed edition of *The Weakest Link*. For that quiz victory she won £11,050 for the charity Sands, which supports people affected by the death of a baby. (In 2006 she had lost her own new-born baby daughter.) *The Weakest Link* triumph was a great moment for the woman that Sugar had told: 'It says here she used to train Financial Directors for MG Rover. No wonder they went bloody skint!' She's a plucky woman and a true survivor, as well as an undoubted *Apprentice* big mouth.

Paul Torrisi

Paul Torrisi was an early *Apprentice* legend, the series-one candidate of whom Lord Sugar said: 'He had many characteristics that reminded me of myself.' A 34-year-old property developer, Paul Torrisi was a glorious entertainment throughout the opening series. It was people such as him who set the precedent for outspoken candidates on the series.

Having also made money selling cars during his life, he carried plenty of the used-car salesman bluster with him into *The Apprentice*. Eminently, endlessly quotable, while selling he had a knack of finding out a detail about a potential customer and then driving home a connection – real or otherwise – with his prey.

'Are you Irish? My wife's Irish!' he said to one would-be customer.

On encountering a decorator, he said: 'My Grandad was a painter and decorator. He painted Buckingham Palace.'

On hearing an east European accent, he asked: 'Are you Polish, Eva? My auntie's Polish!'

Even a member of a highly unpopular profession was not immune to his disingenuous charms: 'Traffic wardens don't get the respect they're due.'

It was all very amusing stuff. Torrisi was as charged and ambitious as *Apprentice* candidates come. Not one to be especially gracious in victory, he celebrated task wins as if they had been achieved in the field of a full battle. 'We utterly demolished the other side,' he said one week, beaming with excitement and joy. 'It was utterly an obliteration.' He often rubbed other candidates up the wrong way, particularly the female of the species. 'Give a woman a position of power and they go fricking doolally,' he said as he waited outside the boardroom one week. 'All of a sudden they're Adolf Flaming Hitler.' During one particularly tense task he screamed and swore at Saira. Challenged on his attitude to women he said: 'I don't have a problem working with women at all, providing they do what they are told!'

In the boardroom, it was clear that Sugar admired Torris's superb salesmanship and some aspects of his driven and rather cheeky persona, but he worried about his temper and other aspects of his personality. 'Are you an arrogant git?' Sugar asked him. 'I'm not,' replied Torrisi, 'but if I'm good at something, I don't mind telling everyone that I'm good at it.' The trouble was he thought he was good at just about everything. However, he found that Sugar was not one to easily fall for his high-volume bluster. As a particularly disastrous task was picked apart, he told Lord Sugar: 'I am a Roman Catholic and as God is my witness I shook her hand outside.' To which Sugar replied memorably: 'Well, I'm Jewish and I couldn't care less.'

Torrisi just couldn't win. When challenged on his noisy manner, he said he attributed it to being Italian. 'That's no excuse for having a temper,' chastised Margaret Mountford in response. When he was finally shown the door he did not meekly stand up and leave the boardroom as most candidates do. Instead he reflected that, throughout his life prior to *The Apprentice*, he didn't know of anyone who had a bad word to say about him but that, throughout the show, he had been widely criticised and hated. 'Why is that?' he asked Sugar. 'Good question – go away and think about it,' replied the boss.

'Well, I've got nothing better to do now, have I?' said Torrisi sadly. It was an almost humble and defeated end to an *Apprentice* journey that had been full of bluster, self-belief and above all – chat. He quickly returned to form in the aftermath, saying: 'It still hurts I didn't get to the last two. Saira and Tim – Asian girl against black kid from east London – it just smacked of the BBC a bit; it annoys me.'

Ruth Badger

Who can forget Ruth Badger? Who would want to? She arrived on the show as a 27-year-old from Wolverhampton with a variety of jobs under her belt. She had worked for a loan company, the Department of Social Security, behind a bar and as a football steward. Just like Lord Sugar, even at school she had shown enterprise, buying erasers and selling them to friends at a profit. 'From a young age money turned me on,' she said. 'I wanted to get out there and make a million.'

She left as the runner-up of series two, but few could believe she had not won the show outright. In between she had cemented a reputation as a formidable saleswoman and a loudmouth extraordinaire. One of her earliest statements on the show made clear that she was not short of words, nor of confidence. 'I don't need a laptop, I don't need a mobile phone, I don't need

THE UNFORGETTABLE RUTH BADGER.

a card,' she said. 'I need me, this mouth, this brain, this body and I can achieve whatever I need to.' During team meetings at the beginning of each task she was focused and brilliantly bossy. Even when she was not team leader, it was often Badger that was pulling the strings.

Her big mouth could close her sales in a range of different ways, from a bawling pitch on a street market to a smooth-talking session on the shop floor. 'She was almost supersonic,' said celebrity *Apprentice* fan Vanessa Feltz, herself not exactly a shrinking violet. 'She was unassailable, there was nothing the woman couldn't sell!' In the boardroom, Badger made for a terrifying opponent who could verbally pound her rival candidates until they whimpered for mercy. She was not going to go down without a fight and she fought wisely.

Even when Lord Sugar put her on the spot, telling her she was a 'one-trick pony', she replied forcefully, listing her achievements and skills. It was not enough to win her the series – she finished runner-up to Michelle Dewberry. Plenty disagreed with that decision. 'Ruth should have won,' was Margaret Mountford's verdict. Many viewers strongly agreed. Badger remains an inspirational figure to would-be business people, perhaps especially women. Not that she is one for automatic 'sisterhood' when it comes to work. 'Last year's female contestants were appalling,' she said ahead of the final. 'They spent their whole time fighting. If we encourage young women to go into business, great, but we're there on our own terms.'

Saira Khan

Who will ever forget series-one runner-up Saira Khan? The 34-year-old sales executive had a BA in Humanities, an MA in Environmental Planning and a big, *big* mouth. She was a very, very talkative and loud lady. 'I came out of my mother's womb competitive,' she said in an opening and characteristically belligerent blast. She has also revealed that her late father told her: 'That gob of yours will get you into trouble'.

In *The Apprentice* it got her all the way to the final. During one sales task, in which she bellowed through a loud hailer, she announced: 'I'm really sorry that I'm very, very loud, but I was born with this gob and I am going to use it.' However, she won the hearts of the public and even of her rival candidates. When Raj was fired instead of her in week nine, he said: 'I'm glad she stayed because she has shined among everyone.'

The bigmouth of series one finished in second place. Summing up the contrast between herself and the winner Tim Campbell, she said: 'I'm not a "yes" person.

If Sir Alan said "jump" to Tim, Tim would say: "how high?" If he said "jump" to me, I'd say: "what for?"' And she would probably say it very, very loudly. It was an ungracious response, but an honest one. She has done her best to stay in the public eye ever since, speaking out about burkhas, our immigration system and other headline-grabbing, attention-ensuring topics.

Syed Ahmed

Ahead of his *Apprentice* journey, Syed Ahmed described himself thus: 'I'm streetwise, I've been a sort of hell-raiser over the past ten years and I think all that combined together has made me a business bad boy.' Once he was on our screens, an online blogger offered his own assessment of this lively candidate: 'Syed could start a fight in an empty house.' Both descriptions were accurate.

Before the show he had spent two years working as a director of his own IT recruitment company with a turnover of £1.6 million. In each *Apprentice* task he participated in, he was rarely far from controversy or conflict. But there was often a nagging suspicion that he had a fan in a high place. When Lord Sugar gave Ahmed a second chance at the end of a feisty boardroom showdown, the candidate said: 'Thank you for the opportunity,' as he left the room. Although

Sugar looked put out by this, some viewers wondered whether he was suppressing a grin of admiration. It was suggested that perhaps he saw a little of himself in the cheeky candidate.

This is more than likely. Although he has never been specific, Lord Sugar has admitted that some candidates have reminded him of himself in his earlier years of business. 'I'm cut from a different cloth and have yet to meet a candidate that is a replication of me, but there are certainly candidates in the past who have shown flashes of me when I was younger,' he said. Combative and opinionated, Ahmed showed plenty of the sort of confidence that got Sugar where he was.

Was there more to Syed than what came across on screen? At the end of one task, Lord Sugar offered him immunity from the firing line because of his impressive salesmanship during the task. This was a rare, golden opportunity to ensure his survival for another week. However, Ahmed was honourable and brave enough to decline the offer of immunity. He voluntarily put himself forward to face the possibility of a firing. Not that viewers were made aware of this – the entire scene was edited out of the final version.

The production team insists there was nothing sinister about this. The series editor, Dan Adamson, said: 'We weren't deliberately making Syed look bad. The scene just didn't fit.' Although he survived that week, he was eventually shown the door and forced to bow out from the process. 'Syed, despite some flashes of genius, you're too much of a risk for me,' said Lord Sugar.

Tre Azam

Tre Azam, like Lord Sugar, grew up in Hackney. He could also give the *Apprentice* boss a run for his money when it came to outspoken opinions. However, some would argue that Azam's self-confidence was not as well justified as the boss's. Indeed, his arrogance bordered on the delusional. Shy and retiring he was not: when he was asked what he had learned from his *Apprentice* experience, Azam replied that it had taught him how many things he was already good at.

Azam was controversial from the start, successfully suggesting the name 'Certus' for the men's team. What he did not mention to his fellow candidates was that this was also the name of a company that had recently employed him. Sir Alan learned of this sly bit of advertising by Azam and let rip at him in front of all the candidates. 'Certus is going to bleeding hurt us today,' roared Sir Alan. 'You've been legged over, boys.' Turning specifically to Azam, he said: 'Your card is marked.' He ordered the team to come-up with a new name and they did so, renaming themselves Eclipse.

Tre Azam.

Eventual series winner Tim Ambrose said of him, 'He wasn't a bullshitter, he was a master bullshitter. He took bullshitting onto the next level.' It was also observed that the words 'team' and 'Tre' could never exist in the same sentence. This was certainly the opinion of week-one team leader Rory who tried to remind Azam: 'I am your boss.' Azam was having none of it: 'You're nothing to me,' he snapped. Later in the series, Azam similarly undermined other team leaders, telling one: 'You're really beginning to piss me off.' He was unyielding in his criticism and targets. When a female contestant disagreed with him he dismissed the matter, saying: 'It's probably her time of the month.'

One writer observed that Tre often looked 'like he's sniffing sour milk'. In fact, he was often in pain during filming, the bitter legacy of a near-fatal car crash ten years earlier. 'I have pain all the time,' he said. When his time on the show came to an end, Lord Sugar told him he was 'argumentative' and 'difficult'. It is safe to say that his experience did nothing to make him more humble. On his personal website, he introduces himself: 'Although a superstar in my own rights, many of you will know me from the BBC Hit Show *The Apprentice*...'

Who could forget him?

BOARDROOM

The boardroom is heart of *The Apprentice*. It is where the firing and – eventually – the hiring takes place. The candidates assemble there at the end of each task and pick over the bones of what took place. It is revealed which team won the task and one of the candidates from the losing team is fired, but not before angry scenes of recrimination, buck-passing and character assassination. It makes for adrenaline-pumping viewing.

The slick, gleaming 'boardroom' is, in fact, a purpose-built television studio on Westfields Road in west London. With up to 19 people sitting round a table and multiple cameras and crew members present, it would be unfeasible to film these scenes in a real-life boardroom. The sessions in the boardroom sometimes go on for several hours. Lord Sugar's decision on who to fire is entirely his own; he does not share his intention with anyone in advance. Nick Hewer has confirmed that not even he is made aware of the plan ahead of its delivery.

Not everything that takes place in the boardroom is quite as sombre and argumentative as it appears on screen. As Lord Sugar wrote in his memoir, *What You See Is What You Get*, there is a lot of humour and banter among the discussions. Such scenes are usually the first to be cut from the show, with angrier exchanges the most likely to survive the cut. 'They are not actually in a torture chamber,' he told BBC Radio 4's *Today* programme.

As the popularity of *The Apprentice* has soared, so has there grown a fascination about the boardroom. In much the same way as the *Big Brother* house has become almost like a character itself, so has the boardroom assumed an identity of its own. In iconic stature it far exceeds that of the titular den of *Dragons' Den*. There has been amused speculation about Lord Sugar's seat, prompted by series-one candidate James Max. After Max was fired, he used the fame he had acquired on the show to launch a media career for himself. Lord Sugar's caustic comment was that Max was a 'pathetic man'. He was to infuriate Sugar even more when he told the media that Sugar's boardroom chair had been placed on top of a box to make him appear taller. A similar claim was made by Jenny Celerier when she was later fired. 'I did notice when he got on to his chair he did do a sort of little jump to get on to it,' she said. Then the *Daily Telegraph* claimed that it had spotted 'a fleeting glimpse' of such a platform.

As Sugar himself acknowledged this story was like 'manna from heaven' for the media, which cause 'a load of aggravation' for the *Apprentice* publicity department. The truth, as Sugar outlines in his memoir, is that his seat was placed in a frame to prevent its wheels sliding around during filming. The decor of the boardroom has become legendary. The *Daily Telegraph* described it as 'aqueous-looking'. An interior-planning website offers a step-by-step guide to making any company boardroom more like the one on *The Apprentice*. When Hiban Ansary was fired from *Junior Apprentice* in 2010, the issue of Sugar's height came up again. 'Lord Sugar was certainly not how I expected,' she said. 'Aside from the fact that he was a lot shorter than I had thought, he was also a lot more approachable and understanding than the television makes him seem.'

After a candidate is fired from the boardroom, they are shown walking into a waiting black cab, which will whisk them off into the night. These 'walks of shame' are not filmed on the same day as the firing. Instead, each candidate is separately filmed on the first day of production and the footage for each candidate added into the relevant episode. Eagle-eyed viewers might have spotted that, particularly in the latter episodes of each series, the fired candidate sometimes has noticeably different hair length as they make the walk of shame.

Similarly, when Katie Hopkins left the boardroom she was wearing a black suit, but when she was shown stepping into the taxi, she was wearing a white suit under a black coat. What actually occurs after the firing is less dramatic and divisive than the on-screen account. The fired contestant and the pair that survived meet up again in an ante-room and have chat over coffee. The receptionist, who sits outside the boardroom and takes Lord Sugar's call asking her to 'send them in, please', is an actress.

No other business show (see THE BUSINESS GENRE) has ever created an environment with anywhere near the degree of the *Apprentice* boardroom. For the ITV show *Tycoon*, Peter Jones sat at a 200kg vintage walnut desk and the contestants parked their behinds on fine office chairs that cost more than £2,000. Yet nobody spoke of those rooms with such revered tones as they quickly did with *The Apprentice*. In the end, Jones did the hiring and firing for *Tycoon* outside the building. Meanwhile, across six series of *The Apprentice*, as well as the charity and Junior spin-offs, the boardroom remains the focal point of the show.

BRIDGE END CAFE

Although it has not quite reached the iconic stature of the Boardroom, the Bridge End Cafe is another venue that has found an unlikely level of fame thanks to its regular appearances on *The Apprentice*. This is the cafe that the losing team is sent to in order to discuss their failed task, as the winning team are setting off on their reward. Their recriminatory presence in the unforgiving surroundings of this transport-style cafe forms an irresistible contrast to the opulent experience that the winning team is simultaneously enjoying. *Apprentice* fanatics have flocked to the humble west London cafe, keen to have a first-hand experience at a regular location.

The owners of the cafe were taken by surprise by the popularity the show brought to their business. It was opened in the 1960s by two Italian brothers, Frank and Gerry Marcangelo. One day, the producers of *The Apprentice* popped in to the cafe and asked the brothers if they could film some scenes there. The brothers said yes but they had no idea how much that decision would change their lives. It was not the first time the cafe has been featured on television. It was featured in the 1960s police drama *Z Cars*. During the 1980s, pop duo Mel & Kim were filmed on the premises and then comedian and author David Baddiel was interviewed on camera there.

However, it was only when their premises began to be featured on *The Apprentice* that their lives and livelihood changed for ever. 'We can't believe it. Business has never been better,' said Frank. The

The Bridge End Cafe's other famous customers include David Baddiel.

downside was that *Apprentice* fans often rang the cafe, to ask if it really was the one featured on the show. 'I don't know what the attraction is, to be honest,' said Gerry. 'People keep coming in and asking: "Is this where they do the *Apprentice*?" They came down from Liverpool to do an article the other day. Must be mad. I can't see it myself.'

Frank, who is more enthusiastic, said that watching the candidates pick over the latest failed task is often akin to watching a production of Punch & Judy. Their regular clientele is dominated by taxi drivers and labourers, but now they had suited young business hopefuls arriving, with a camera crew. 'It is funny to see these young City types in their sharp suits shouting about who did what,' he said. 'Sometimes I just close my ears and wish they would hush their noise.' He said that the candidates were a mixed breed, but most were pleasant and admirable. It was always amusing to see the more posh and dapper candidates in this working-men's cafe, most notably Raef, who sat ill at ease in the venue while urging his team-mates to show 'solidarity, camaraderie and truth'.

The food on sale at Bridge End Cafe has not changed much over the decades. 'What the working man wanted to eat 50 years ago, they still eat today,' explained Gerry. They have experimented with salad and fancy coffees, but have found that neither really took off. The trade is in their blood, when their Italian grandfather first came to England he ran a number of cafes. He had the sort of hard-working, entrepreneurial spirit that Lord Sugar would surely have admired.

Gerry's daughter has shown a bit of it herself. She suggested to her father that they produce some special mugs, with 'You're Fired' emblazoned across them. Others have mooted the idea of the cafe creating a commemorative 'Apprentice Breakfast'. However, Gerry rejected both ideas, saying he was 'too old and miserable' to go down that line. He also said he found Lord Sugar 'a bit of a turn-off' and that, when he watched him on *Celebrity Who Wants To Be A Millionaire*, he thought he came across 'a bit dim'. It takes a brave man to speak so damningly of Lord Sugar.

THE BUSINESS GENRE

The success of *The Apprentice* has created a whole school of programming in the shape of shows clearly influenced by its format. But none of them have managed to surpass *The Apprentice* and some flopped spectacularly.

ITV introduced *Tycoon*, fronted by Peter Jones, the

Saira Khan presented *Beat the Boss*.

telecommunications magnate made famous by the BBC2 series *Dragons' Den*. Launched on ITV in June 2007, *Tycoon* featured six budding entrepreneurs who brought a business idea to the show. At the end of each show, a contestant was removed from the line-up by Jones. One of the differences between *Tycoon* and *The Apprentice* was that the winner was chosen by a public vote, rather than by Jones. This populist edge actually rather confused the format of the show, which fell strangely between two themes. It drew disappointing ratings and after just two weeks was moved to a less mainstream slot. The original 60-minute episodes were then reduced to 30-minute shows. Lord Sugar said it 'bombed'.

Beat the Boss was launched in 2006 as a children's television show on the BBC. It was co-presented by businessman Cameron Johnson and *Apprentice* graduate Saira Kahn. Two teams (one made up of children, one by adults) compete to create a product that would appeal to children. In 2008, the BBC broadcast a children's political reality show called *Election*. Two teams of contestants undertake politically-themed challenges such as debating, diplomacy and campaigning. The losing team faces Jonathan Dimbleby, who selects one candidate to leave the process, telling them: 'Your campaign is over,' a political twist on the famous 'You're fired' of *The Apprentice*. Among the mentors who guided the candidates through their tasks was *Apprentice* series two winner Michelle Dewberry.

There have also been satirical parodies of *The Apprentice*. Harry Hill's *TV Burp* has often made fun of the show, as has *Dead Ringers* with scenes in which Lord Sugar turns fired candidates into frogs, and *Bremner Bird & Fortune*, with a London Mayoral election-themed sketch. A website called 'Bolegbros' has produced a spoof of the show using Lego characters. All these parodies have been great fun, and further evidence of the success and influence of *The Apprentice*.

> ### DID YOU KNOW?
> *Tycoon* drew 2 million viewers for episode one, but dropped 100,000 of those for episode two. ITV normally expects to grab an average of 4.5million viewers for that slot.

BUYING TASKS

During each series of *The Apprentice*, the candidates have been set a 'buying' task. They are handed a list of ten unrelated items to buy at the lowest possible price. They are penalised for any items they fail to purchase and the team that spends least money wins. It sounds simple on paper, doesn't it? Anyone who has watched these tasks knows that they prove a testing hurdle.

This is not least because the list of items always includes a few 'curve-balls' – obscure, mysteriously-named items which the candidates have never heard of. Given that they are not allowed to use the internet during the task, just finding out what some of the items are proves a challenge. (Indeed, one candidate told *The Times* that they are even followed to the toilet by production staff during tasks, to ensure they do not break any rules whilst spending a penny. Their shoes are also searched to ensure they are not concealing money.)

From the start, the buying task has proved one of the more testing challenges. Given the concrete, black-and-white target, candidates who had previously blown a lot of hot air to get by would suddenly struggle. Often a simple item on the list would throw them wildly off course. In the first series, one team failed to purchase a bowler hat, one of the more straightforward products on the list. The following year, team Velocity didn't buy the tyre on the list and lost the task by just £8. With the teams

RAEF BJAYOU WITH PRINCE CHARLES.

battling against the clock, it's no surprise that some things slip through the net.

Each year, the challenge has become harder. In series three, the item on the list that most puzzled the contestant was Nigella seeds. These are seeds that are often found in naan bread, but the candidates had no idea what they were, nor were they allowed to use the internet to find out. Adam Hosker became gripped by the idea that Nigella seeds were something to do with astro-turf pitches that footballers sometimes play on. It seemed an unlikely prospect, but that did not prevent him phoning an astro-turf company to grill them. 'What are they called, those granules? Those little rubber bits on the new kinds of astroturf?' He was told that the rubber granules are in fact called... 'rubber granules'. Not to be beaten by facts, he double-checked that the rubber granules are not in fact known as Nigella seeds. It was a terrible task for Adam, who was shown the door by Lord Sugar at the end of it after his team lost the task by just 97 pence.

In series four the margin of victory was bigger but still not huge: Alpha beat Renaissance by £35.99, after a task memorable mostly for the KOSHER CHICKEN debacle. In series six, the trickiest item on the list was something that seemed simple enough at first glance – a four-metre kitchen worktop. However,

APPRENTICE CONTESTANT KATIE HOPKINS.

this was a challenge too far for Jamie Lester, who spent many frustrating – but for the audience, entertaining – hours trying to obtain one. 'This kitchen worktop is haunting me,' he sighed after once more failing to find one. So legendary did his futile quest become that, when he later appeared on the *You're Fired* show, he was given as his going-home present a four-metre kitchen worktop. Throughout the series it has been amusing to see the wild-goose chases the candidates go on, as well as the shameless flirtation that female candidates are sometimes willing to employ in order to drive a price down.

No wonder the buying-task round has become so popular among *Apprentice* fans. As well as the above difficulties faced by contestants, there have also been some impressive moments. In series one Saira and Raj managed to obtain one of the items on the list (a television Freeview box) absolutely free. This contributed to their team's victory. Despite being haunted by the kitchen worktop in series six, Jamie Lester negotiated imaginatively, hard and effectively. For instance, he purchased the mysterious 22-carat gold tikka (an Indian headdress) for a bargain £135.

However, it will always be the disasters that live longest in the memory. As Lord Sugar told team Impact at the end of the very first buying task: 'You've given me so many excuses, you remind me of my football managers. In fact, you've taught them a few tricks!' The legacy of his football career lives on.

C is for...

CAT CALENDARS

Pitching is a key part of business and *The Apprentice* regularly tests people's ability to present their ideas. Sometimes, this leads to some awe-inspiring, attention-grabbing pitches. Occasionally, it leads to a disaster. For instance, in series one Rachel threw her shoes around the room and danced during her presentation, much to the horror of the assembled industry luminaries. However, the most enduring, disastrous and toe-curling example of a poor pitch came when the teams were set the task of producing fundraising calendars to pitch to three retailers. For the men's team, Mani pitched pretty badly. However, so poor were their rival team's pitches that they got away with it.

The girls were led by project manager Nargis Aga, who had claimed at the outset of the series that presentation was her strong point. 'I speak clearly, I bring my level up or down depending on whom I'm speaking to,' she said. Therefore, she insisted on doing the pitching on the day. When she pitched their cat-calendar idea to three leading retailers, she could hardly have got it more wrong. As the watching Ruth Badger later put it, this was so embarrassing and terrible a pitch, she wanted to 'crawl up my own backside'.

Far from charming those she pitched to, she actually interrupted them right from the first pitch.

Nargis: 'Ask me any questions...'

Retailer: 'What sort of retail price do you—'

Nargis: 'I haven't finished speaking, sorry. Ask me any questions that you have and then let's talk about how many you want.'

As Nick Hewer described this opening pitch: 'It was the most horrible two or three minutes of a pitch I have ever, ever seen.' But there were further cringes to come as she finally stopped talking and accepted a question.

Retailer: 'What sort of cost price do you imagine?'

After a lengthy pause, Nargis: 'Er, sorry, can you repeat the question?'

Retailer: 'What sort of cost price... do you imagine?'

For the final pitch of the day, Nargis again decided that interrupting the retailer was a sensible way to build a rapport.

Her pitch seemed to come to an end when she looked at the retailer and told him: 'This product will look great on your shelves.' After waiting a few seconds, he said: 'Ok, I've got a couple of questions,' only to be interrupted by Aga. 'Oh, there's more,' he said, with a deflated air. So what was *so* important for her to say, that it was worth interrupting the man she was pitching to? 'Now you can ask me any questions,' she said, 'and then let's talk about how many you want to buy.' Naturally, the retailer rolled his eyes.

Back in the boardroom, Nargis attempted to defend herself. 'I think I negotiated well,' she said. Sir Alan disagreed. 'Nargis, you're fired,' he said.

CHEESE

It is a foodstuff that has baffled, troubled and derailed the progress of *Apprentice* candidates on more than one occasion. Scientists have claimed that cheese can give those who eat it late at night vivid nightmares. It has certainly proved a nightmare on Britain's biggest business show, and never more so than in episode six of series three, when Sir Alan sent the candidates the tricky task of selling British food in a French street market. Former Army Lieutenant Paul Callaghan made the puzzling decision to buy a huge quantity of low-price cheddar from a cash-and-carry, in the hope that French cheese connoisseurs would snap it up.

For many viewers this plan was bonkers and

MANI SANDHER, RUTH BADGER, ANSELL HENRY AND SAYED AHMED.

perilously similar to trying to sell coal to Newcastle. Explaining his peculiar tactic, Callaghan said he took a deliberate gamble having become frustrated with the lack of cavalier spirit that had been on display so far in the series. 'Everyone had been playing it so safe and I either wanted to win big or lose big,' he said. The result was that he lost big: his team made a £225.84 loss, while their opponents turned a profit of £410. It was '*au revoir*' for Paul, who had previously been earmarked as a potential winner by Lord Sugar, Nick Hewer and Margaret Mountford.

In the aftermath of this memorable episode, a British cheese manufacturer set out to prove that British cheese can sell in France. Representatives of Wyke Farms in Somerset took some of their finest cheddar to a French market and quickly sold out of their stock. Managing Director Richard Clothier was bullish when he announced this success to the media. He said: 'Alan Sugar, you know a lot about electronics, but not that much about cheese and, for that reason, you're fired!'

It had proved a useful counter-strategy public relations-wise, but most people would still argue that selling cheap cheese to the French is a fool's errand. But Makro cheese buyer Andy Walsh was not to be bowed. He, too, launched a thundering public-relations bid to rebut the perceptions created by the cheese task. 'British cheeses are increasingly popular in France – with sales rising by twenty per cent year on year,' he said. 'Where the contestants on *The Apprentice* failed is not with the quality of the product they were offering, but by not realising that the key to selling to the French is to appeal to their taste buds. They don't care about packaging or brand names – what they want is to try the food – and once they've tried it, they invariably like it and will buy it.'

In the opening episode of series one of *Junior Apprentice*, the young candidates were given the challenge of selling fine cheeses to the people of London. Adam Eliaz, a cocky 17-year-old Londoner, announced that he would focus his efforts on females as, he concluded: 'Women love cheese.' Given what a calorie-packing foodstuff cheese is, his theory seemed flawed, but his charm worked wonders and he managed to shift a fair amount of cheese. The boys' team finished runners-up to the girls, but Eliaz escaped the boardroom chop. Soon after this he fell ill and was sent home.

In the second episode of series five of the main *Apprentice* show there was a further *fromage* flop when Geordie Rocky Andrews lost money during a catering challenge, despite his experience of running successful sandwich shops. The task was to cater for city

NEVER KNOWINGLY UNDER-CHICKENED – SYED AMED.

stockbrokers and, when Andrews' Empire team offered them cheese and pickle on a cocktail stick, they were unimpressed. 'They will want the best they can imagine,' said Nick Hewer of the client-base, 'and what are they getting? They're getting cheddar on a stick!' Put like that, it did seem a meagre offering.

Lord Sugar sent Andrews packing, saying: 'One cannot ignore what I call immature mistakes.' The 21-year-old candidate was truly cheesed off by this and claimed his dismissal was a result of a southern bias on the part of Lord Sugar. 'It's no surprise, there was me and two southerners in the boardroom,' he said. 'I respect Sir Alan but at the end of the day he's a southerner and he always seems to employ southerners.' Was this more like sour grapes than fine *fromage*?

Other cheese-related slip-ups included episode four of series two when Alexa's Invicta team ordered the ingredients to make a hundred chicken tikka pizzas. They had, on the suggestion of Syed Ahmed, ordered a hundred chickens for these. 'So that's... one chicken per pizza?' asked an incredulous Nick Hewer as the candidates began to appreciate the scale of the 'fowl-up' they had committed. This cock-up was made worse when the chickens arrived — they were the size of turkeys, compounding the error.

The mix-up was especially galling because Syed Ahmed had long billed himself to his fellow candidates as something of a restaurant expert. Their belief in this melted faster than a pizza in an oven as their chicken-tikka disaster became clear. 'Yes, we are in the shit,' said Ahmed. 'We need to find a solution.' That was an understatement. 'We don't know what we're doing at the moment,' observed team-mate Tuan, hitting the nail on the head. Alexa was shown the door after Invicta lost the task, another candidate to fall foul of the curse of cheese. It has 'stilton' many an *Apprentice* journey.

COMIC RELIEF DOES THE APPRENTICE

Between series two and three of *The Apprentice*, fans got an extra helping of the show in the form of a celebrity version, which raised funds for the Comic Relief charity.

Series One

The programme pit five famous men against five famous women. The male team was comprised of actor Ross Kemp, broadcaster Danny Baker, spin doctor Alastair Campbell, actor Rupert Everett and celebrity journalist Piers Morgan. The women's team was made up of pop star Cheryl Cole, comedian Jo Brand, actress

CHARLIE BURDEN

Comic Relief Apprentice Ross Kemp.

Maureen Lipman, fashion broadcaster Trinny Woodall and business woman Karren Brady. Their task was to run a funfair in London and invite high-spending celebrity guests to roll-up and spend bags of money. The team that raised most money (for Comic Relief) would win.

Proceedings proved unpredictable from the start. Lord Sugar's attempts at humour in the initial boardroom meeting fell flat. He admits in his memoir that recalling that scene makes him 'cringe'. The knowledge that rom-com director and Comic Relief boss Richard Curtis was watching proceedings only made Sugar's comfort lessen. However, things were going to get even less comfortable when Everett decided that the process was not for him. He decided to leave the show, which he declared as 'too *Big Brother*'. He also had a moan about Lord Sugar, saying: 'That guy, Sir Donald Sugarbeet or whatever he was called was so hideous. He looks like Sid James.' He was replaced – at the suggestion of Margaret Mountford – by series one *Apprentice* winner, Tim Campbell. He brought some added business nous to the men's team, but it was the ladies that would laugh last and loudest.

With future *Apprentice* board member Karren Brady at the helm, they cleverly raised nearly a quarter of a million pounds. Woodall in particular utilised some vital contacts to bring in large sums. As Brand later commented: 'Trinny Woodall knows everyone in Belgravia who earns more than £10 million a year so she got on the phone and the rest of us just went to the pub, it was great!' With the women declared the winners, Sugar had to decide which of the men to 'fire'. He ended up choosing Morgan – who was fired by the *Daily Mirror* in 2004 – for the walk of shame, citing the fact that the former tabloid editor had been cantankerous and provocative throughout the process. When he told Morgan: 'You're fired', Campbell jokingly said to Morgan: 'Again?!'

However, in truth Morgan was one of the true winners of the show. Having left tabloid journalism behind seemingly for good, he was keen to become a television celebrity himself. His only success to date was on the ill-fated Channel 4 current affairs show *Morgan & Platell*. Thanks to his attention-grabbing performance on *Comic Relief Does The Apprentice*, he began to be seen as a more mainstream television prospect. As did Cheryl Cole. It is no coincidence that both ended up as judges on Simon Cowell-run reality shows in the wake of their appearance on the charity *Apprentice*. More importantly, between them the two teams had raised over £1million pounds for Comic Relief.

Series Two

The men's team included: comedians Alan Carr and Jack Dee, broadcaster Jonathan Ross, businessman Gerald Ratner and celebrity stylist Gok Wan. For the women we had broadcasters Carol Vorderman, Ruby Wax and Fiona Phillips, businesswoman Michelle Mone and *EastEnders* actress Patsy Palmer. The task was to create a toy and then market it at an industry show.

There was extra attention on this series, due to the presence of Jonathan Ross, who was at the time suspended from the BBC after his part in the telephone prank played on elderly actor Andrew Sachs. He had been allowed to take part because it was a previously agreed charitable venture, which partially helped lift the ratings to 7.94 million (from 6.72 million in the first series).

The general sense of controversy did not end with Ross. Lord Sugar complained about the 'egos' and said it was a 'bloody joke'. He nearly walked out at one stage and after the filming had finished declared that this was the last time he would take part in a celebrity version of *The Apprentice*. Behind the scenes, he added, the production team were 'tearing their hair out' with frustration. He was not the only participant to threaten to walk during the production. Palmer had a silly row with team leader Mone, a disagreement which Wax

Comic Relief second series Apprentice Alan Carr.

would describe as 'barbaric'. The actress announced she was quitting the filming, but her husband convinced her to return. When Mone was made team leader for the ladies, she had warned her team-mates: 'You'll hate me! I'm a *psycho*!'

Meanwhile, the men's team was a more harmonious unit. The only discord was a bit of comic squabbling between Dee and Ross. However, for the second time it was the men who ended up losing the task after Mone's ladies created the more profitable product. The ensuing final boardroom was once more a humorous affair, particularly when Dee suggested to Lord Sugar that he fire adviser Nick Hewer. In the end it was Alan Carr that faced the bullet. Carr later slammed Sugar during an interview with *new!* magazine. 'Just how scary is he? He's horrible. I thought because we were celebrities he'd tone it down, but he was vile and laid into me. I used to take the mickey out of the contestants when they cried on *The Apprentice*, but he had me in tears. I was gulping and had a lump in my throat!'

At the time of writing there are no known plans for further spin-offs along the lines of the above. However, in March 2011, the candidates from series six of the main *Apprentice* show undertook a special sponsored challenge involving tunnels, rope swings, high walls, water obstacles and barbed wire. All the money raised went to Comic Relief.

CREDIT CRUNCH

In the summer of 2007, two previously rarely-spoken terms became common currency in conversations across the globe. As the 'credit crunch' took hold, it quickly became a full-on 'financial meltdown'. These were uncertain times for all and, as the economic crisis caused much hardship, programmes such as *The Apprentice* had to reconsider their approach. It suddenly seemed inappropriate to be discussing big money and get-rich schemes in front of audiences who were scared for their own financial futures.

Not that Lord Sugar was about to rein in his usual blunt chat when discussing the issue. 'I don't know what everybody's moaning about,' he told an interviewer for the *Daily Telegraph*. It's all nonsense about recession and all that stuff. Absolute total nonsense. Because I started my business in 1967 in a recession and I started it without having to go to banks and get loans. There's an expectancy culture that the Government's got to do something for you, the bank's got to do something for you, that it's all laid on. If it was all as easy as that, we'd all be Richard Bransons and Philip Greens and Alan Sugars.'

A FEARSOME
BOARDROOM
LINE-UP.

Brave words, especially considering the outrage that has greeted other public figures who have spoken in similar terms about the financial climate. He was not to be cowed, though. 'I think it's a cushy society at the moment,' he said. 'Everyone has two cars, two tellies, one microwave and lots of benefits. They can't be bothered to work.' On a less contentious and more inspirational note, he has contended that even the worst business disasters have their positive points. 'Some of the greatest entrepreneurs and billionaires are actually people who have gone bust; failure is a way of learning' he said.

For series six, candidates were selected to reflect the harsh realities of the time. Alex Epstein was an unemployed communications head, while Raleigh Addington was a university graduate who had yet to find work. 'The economic situation has seen many people being made redundant or seen their businesses fail through no fault of their own,' explained Lord Sugar in more understanding tones. 'They're very capable people and we thought we'd look for a few of those people and give them an opportunity. Failure is part of a learning curve and these people need a chance. We tried to prove it can be possible to come through it and be a winner.'

The Apprentice, at least in its UK form, had never been

an especially greedy or gauche television show. Therefore, it did not need much tinkering in the light of the financial crisis. All the same, the small, finely-tuned changes it did make were important and helped show once more how enduring the programme is. 'I think what we tried to do was encapsulate the economic climate and find people who have been made redundant for example. We've given people another chance and there's a newcomer from university who's found it very difficult to find a job.' Times change, but *The Apprentice* adapts and lives on.

D is for...

DAMNATION

It has won awards, millions of dedicated fans and praise from the critics, but there is no escaping the fact that *The Apprentice* has not been to everyone's taste. The passion of those who have cheered for *The Apprentice* is matched by that of those who dismiss it. Writing in The *Independent*, Terence Blacker argued that the programme was a relic from the past. Given its 'grabby obsession with money and the trappings it brings, the show might more accurately be renamed *The Dinosaur*,' he wrote. Blacker added that the qualities *The Apprentice* promoted were negative: 'Selfishness, a lack of personal accountability, a ruthless aggression towards others.'

Steve Carter, the head of the leading recruitment firm Nigel Lynn, said that the selection process on *The Apprentice* bore little resemblance to the real world of employment. 'The idea that people should set about stabbing each other in the back to succeed is not good business,' he said. 'It's sheer sensationalism,' added Alison Hodgson, chair of the Association of Graduate Recruiters. 'Highly entertaining and nothing more than that.' Some commentators contrasted *The Apprentice* in this sense with *Dragons' Den*, which for a few years included a leading recruitment expert, James Caan, in its number.

There was some justification in their argument that the show does not precisely mirror the real business world. Neither does it claim to, though. It is indeed an entertainment show when all is said and done. Indeed, Lord Sugar himself has been quite clear that the show stands outside the experiences of most established business folk. 'To be fair, I've often said, if I was to take some of the leading businessmen in this country and wake them up at six o'clock in the morning and say to them, "you're going out to make some sausages in a factory and you've got to go buy some meat then you've got to sell it in a festival and by six o'clock you've got to be back here," they would fail,' he said. 'They would not know what to do because you've given them a deadline and a timeline and taken them out of their comfort zone.'

In 2007, there were allegations that *The Apprentice* was involved with product placement. The campaigning group Media Watch observed that car manufacturer Chrysler, health spa Champneys and retailer Pets at Home were all featured during that year's series. Talkback Thames strongly denied they had indulged in product placement and insisted any featuring of real-life products was editorially justified. Given the nature of the programme as a business- and commerce-based affair, it is, if anything, remarkable how little presence there is of real-life brands.

Former contestants have also been known to turn on *The Apprentice* on occasion. Saira Khan claimed that the way Lord Sugar is portrayed on screen was reminiscent of a bully, an inflammatory allegation by any standards. 'With Sir Alan, because of the way he is and the language he uses, they're all the characteristics of a bully,' she said, though she was quick to add that she did not believe him to be a bully in real life. Beret-wearing, harp-playing, aromatherapy-using candidate Lucinda Ledgerwood claimed she was treated unfairly by the male candidates. 'On occasions, it was verging on bullying,' she said.

Tre Azam, meanwhile, claimed that footage had been selectively edited to portray him unfairly. As always, the bigmouth was straight to the point in his complaint. 'I am worried that they might have made me out to be a c★★★ at the end of the day,' he told the *Daily Star*. 'I've been exploited like a motherf★★★er but it's all good as it's for TV.' Candidates to make similar complaints about the editing process included Syed Ahmed and Gerri Blackwood. Dan Adamson, an *Apprentice* editor, maintained that editing is fair and that 'Sir Alan, especially,' would never allow it to be otherwise. Series-three winner Simon Ambrose tried to settle the matter when he said of the editing: 'It's unfair and they do cheat a little bit. But they don't misrepresent people or say things happened that didn't happen.'

Someone who would contest Ambrose's claim is Mani Sandher. He complained to the BBC about the editing of episode two of series two, in which he had been shown pitching a calendar to retailers. 'I strongly believe that the editing of episode two [of last year's *Apprentice*] goes against the values of the BBC,' he said. He claimed that the quality of his pitch had been unfairly represented in the final cut and went as far as claiming he had a text message from a series producer which suggested as much.

Sandher said: 'All of the occasions I was criticised by

SERIES-THREE WINNER SIMON AMBROSE.

my team were kept in full in the final edit ... a fair and truthful representation [should] show any counter evidence proving ... I had ... considered pricing.' However, both the BBC editorial-complaints unit and the BBC Trust declined to uphold his complaint. The programme's commissioning executive wrote to Sandher, explaining that 700 hours of footage were recorded and then condensed into 12 hours for the series itself, so the 'programme is not a detailed second-by-second account of reality'.

Interestingly, Lord Sugar himself has complained about some editing. For the second series of *Comic Relief Does The Apprentice*, the trailer stitched together a number of clips that showed him angry or speaking rudely. He had not been shown the trailer before it was broadcast and was furious when he saw it. 'I am the villain all the time,' he told The *Mirror*. 'The idiot that edited it – and I don't know who's done it – went through the past five years of archive to find snapshots of me roaring like a deranged lunatic and just stuck them all together.' Speaking of the saga as 'a dirty trick', he threatened to quit the show if there was any repeat of it. Having fired so many candidates over six years of *The Apprentice*, it would have been an irony if Sugar had pointed at himself and said: "You've quit." Fortunately, peace quickly broke out.

Lord Sugar has also on occasion directly bitten back at those who have damned him. When *Newsnight* host Jeremy Paxman said *The Apprentice* was full of 'know-alls' who had 'nothing to say', Sugar responded with a challenge. 'That's the pot talking to the kettle, isn't it? I mean, he's the most unpleasant person going,' he said. 'I'd like to get into a debate, without him having a day to think up questions to make people seem awkward. I'd like to see how clever he is then. Jeremy Paxman has never interviewed me. I've never met him. But I'd like to be thrown in a room with him to debate something someone throws at us rather than him having a crib sheet hiding under the table. In my opinion that is cheating, honestly.'

Criticism – some of it little more than banter, some of it more aggressive than that – has also come the way of *The Apprentice* from fellow BBC television reality show *Dragons' Den*. Lord Sugar has done nothing to invite criticism from that quarter. 'I love it, I leap out of my chair, especially when someone brings on something electronic, I'm screaming, "I don't invest!"' However, the harsh words were soon being volleyed from the den to the boardroom. 'I don't know how old Sir Alan is, but he must be seventy or seventy-five at least,' said Peter Jones.

It was Jones's fellow dragon Theo Paphitis who really

put the boot in. He said: 'I used to watch *The Apprentice*, but it's become *Big Brother*. They all live in a house together and are given tasks – where do you recognise that? I don't think it's challenging any more. I like Alan Sugar. I think he's fabulous. But the whole format and the things that the contestants do ... It's not a million miles away from what happens in *Big Brother*, which isn't the most intellectually stimulating programme.' Michael Parkinson was also scathing: 'I have an aversion to that programme. When [Sugar] tells someone "You're fired," what's funny about that? You're fired. There's nothing funny about that.'

Eamonn Holmes truly took the gloves off when he launched a fearsome attack on the programme in November 2010. 'I'd hate to think my children could be as poisoned, ruthless and blinkered as the fools on that programme,' he said. 'I think this idolisation we have of business people is wrong. In society we have envy everywhere. Meanness is a trait I despise. That's what I see in *The Apprentice*. It promotes evilness and greed.' One might counter that the undoubted prevalence of envy would not be reduced by the disappearance of *The Apprentice*.

Final word goes to Australian newspaper, *The Age*, which commented of the UK show when it was broadcast Down Under: 'Sir Alan Sugar doesn't have as

DRAGON DEN'S THEO PAPHITIS.

interesting hair as Donald Trump.' A case of praising with faint damnation?

DONALD TRUMP

Before the British version of *The Apprentice* hit our screens, there was already a hugely successful American version. It was the first instalment of the *Apprentice* franchise. Launched by the NBC channel in the winter of 2004, the prize for the winner was a $250,000 starting contract of running one of the companies owned by the show's star, the billionaire Donald Trump. The gruff property and casino magnate was the perfect choice to anchor the show, in which an unflinching focal point was needed. This, after all, is the man who declares himself 'not a big fan of the handshake', reasoning: 'I think it's barbaric, shaking hands. You catch colds, you catch the flu, you catch this, you catch all sorts of things.' The show was a hit from the off, drawing over 20 million viewers each week.

It has run for ten seasons and become a hugely popular part of the American television calendar. One person who is not a fan of the American *Apprentice* is Lord Sugar, who has said he thought it was 'crap'. Explaining why he thought the British one was better, he said: 'There's less glitz and showbiz here. You can follow what's going on. The American one – the business side – was very hard to follow.' The rivalry of business knows no boundaries. 'When you're on a winner, you stick to the winner,' added Sugar. 'You polish it and enhance it and try to make it more interesting to the public ... [the American version] made the fatal error of trying to change things just for the sake of it and it backfired.'

Donald Trump's version has gone through multiple format changes. It also employs *Big Brother*-style gimmicks and mind games, including one year when one of the teams was asked to live in the garden of the house. In contrast, the British *Apprentice* is notable for being arguably the most consistent reality-television format on the airwaves. The series editor said they 'tweak at most', and live by the motto that each series should still feel like the familiar *Apprentice*, 'but better'. Blissfully absent from the mix are any gimmicks.

Lord Sugar would not have had it any other way. However, there were rumours for a while that Trump might be the boss for the UK show as well. As Channel 4 and BBC2 both bid for the UK rights in April 2004, the television trade magazine *Broadcast* reported that Trump was in the frame to be in the chair. However, the seat went to Lord Sugar and he has never shown any sign of wanting to vacate it. He has made a catty

DONALD TRUMP WITH WIFE MELANIA.

remark about his American equivalent, Trump. During his appearance on BBC2 show *Room 101*, Sugar recounted a funny joke he had made at the expense of Trump. It centred on a day when he and a crew were filming footage for the opening titles of *The Apprentice* on a speedboat on the Thames. 'I said to [the crew], "Trump couldn't do this," and they said, "Why not?" and I said, "Cos his bloody hair would be back there at Tower Bridge."'

The two bosses have been compared directly after the British version of *The Apprentice* was shown on American television. Starting in August 2008, it was shown on CNBC on Monday evenings. The following year it moved to BBC America. From the off, the British version had its fans Stateside. The *Baltimore Sun* said: 'Everything I hate about NBC's *The Apprentice*, I like in *The Apprentice: UK*, the Brit version. Self-made rich guy Sir Alan Sugar makes Donald Trump seem like a wimp.'

P.S: 2008 also saw the UK *Apprentice* launched on Australian television. Sugar went down a treat with the straight-talking Aussie public, right from its launch in which Channel 7 marketing girls took to the streets to hand out packets of lollipops with a sticker on the packet that read: 'Alan Sugar... Sweet by name, not by nature.' The press loved him, with the *Sunday Mail* trumpeting: 'Move over Donald Trump – Alan Sugar is in the boardroom and he's far more entertaining.' The same article also spoke with delight and admiration of Sugar's boardroom belligerence: 'Sugar goes totally mental. Fantastic!' The reviewer for the *Townsville Bulletin* was also a fan: 'I gave Sir Alan a chance to impress... let's just say that he had me at, "I don't know if you're just a bloody nutter." There's an undeniably roguish charm about this latest reality TV star which makes *The Apprentice: UK* fascinating viewing.'

E is for...

EDINBURGH

The Margaret Mountford highlight of series four came when she, Lord Sugar and Nick Hewer discussed candidate Michael Sophocles and the fact that he did not seem to understand what a kosher chicken is. Hewer observed: 'It defies belief. He did classics at Edinburgh. He's a bright boy. How could he make such a mess of it?' Mountford's reply was simple, but the gentle, withering exasperation she delivered it with earned it a place in television history. 'Well,' she began, 'I think Edinburgh isn't what it used to be.'

As this response became an instant hit among the

fans, the University's press office issued a rebuttal. It issued a statement pointing out it was 'regularly ranked among the top fifty universities in the world and is currently going through a period of unprecedented growth'. The Edinburgh offence was not enough to stop *The Apprentice* winning the 2009 Media Guardian Edinburgh International TV Festival's Terrestrial Programme of the Year award.

EPISODES

There is a neat symmetry to the episodic structure of *The Apprentice*. Each of the first 12 series have consisted of 12 episodes. This makes it stand apart from other reality shows such as *The X Factor* and *Big Brother*, which regularly altered the number of episodes in each new series.

F is for...

FINAL

The climax of the series sees the final two (or in some cases four) candidates go head to head in a special challenge. At the end of the show Lord Sugar will reveal who he will hire as his next apprentice. It is truly exciting stuff. To add to the climactic atmosphere, many of the candidates who have been fired during the series return to assist the finalists. This dimension of the episode brings up an entertaining scene in which each finalist takes a turn to pick candidates to join their team. It is always painful for those chosen last to realise they are least popular. The whole scene is reminiscent of the day at school when the two sports captains pick their teams. A lovely, ego-stroking experience for those picked first, something akin to hell for those at the lower end of the list.

Then, it is on to the final task. Both finalists will have previously project-led a task, but never have they felt more pressure and responsibility. Not that what occurs in the last task is fully do-or-die stuff. Although both finalists are naturally extremely keen to win the final battle, Lord Sugar does not make his decision as to the winner of the series based only on the last task. Rather, he looks over the entire series to assess the candidate most suited to becoming his next apprentice. Not that this reduces the sense of pressure and destiny during the final task of the series. They have never been anything other than riveting.

Series one final task: To organise and manage a successful party on a Thames riverboat

Tim and Saira were both given £5,000 to fund their event, which they had two days to organise and promote. Tim's event was a fashion evening on a modern river cruiser; Saira arranged a wine-launch on an old-fashioned paddle steamer. Predictably, Tim's project management proved more smooth and diplomatic than Saira's. However, Saira made her £800 while Tim made zero profit.

All the same, as Lord Sugar later wrote, Tim 'showed me aspects of his business nature that I hadn't seen before and demonstrated his potential by taking a longer term, strategic approach to profit. He had considered other ways of making money from the event that would also lead to future business. His attention to detail was impressive – there was no doubt he had the loyalty and goodwill of his team.'

Series two final task: To organise and manage an evening event at London's Tower Bridge

As in series one, the candidate who was hired after the final was the one that technically failed the final task. Ruth Badger chose to run a 'murder-mystery' evening. Her wisely chosen team worked hard and well at selling tickets for the event, guaranteeing a great turn-out on the night. When Lord Sugar made his customary dramatic appearance at the event, he criticised her for a lack of originality in some areas. But it had been an impressive event.

Michelle Dewberry opted for a James Bond-themed casino night, called 'Double-O Heaven'. Her team did not work as harmoniously or effectively as Ruth's, not least because it included the fiery Syed Ahmed in its ranks. Despite a hurried re-arranging of the team, it was hard for Michelle to bounce back and she soon had to

FINALISTS ON *THE APPRENTICE* MIGHT ONE DAY HOPE TO GET THEIR HANDS ON A SUGAR-ESQUE ROLLER.

slash ticket prices for her event from £65 to £10. Badger was the more impressive in this task, but Dewberry was hired thanks to Sugar's belief she performed better over the series.

Her first task as apprentice was to launch a new business called Xenon Green, disposing of companies' unwanted computer equipment. Hers was not to be a successful or lasting apprenticeship, as you can read in WINNERS.

Series three final task: Develop and pitch a proposal for the redevelopment of the IBM building on London's South Bank

Moving away from the more social-themed tasks of the finals for series one and two, this time Lord Sugar charged the top two with a more gritty and imaginative task. It also provided him, in his introduction to it, with the chance to reveal that he had bought the site in question for £120 million. It had been a sweet day for him when he bought the IBM Building, not least because he had once failed a test to become a computer programmer for IBM.

Simon's idea was for a building called 'The Wave', a design that some people jokingly described as being somewhat phallic in appearance. Meanwhile, Kristina opted for a design known as 'The Phoenix', her detailed proposal suggesting a 64 per cent/36 per cent residential/commercial mix including 507 apartments. The plans had interesting contrasts, setting the stage for a fascinating showdown as they approached their presentations.

They pitched their ideas to a 100-strong audience of specially invited property, architecture and financial experts. Both candidates pitched well but it was Simon who came into his own, delivering his pitch in engrossing fashion. As Lord Sugar put it, Simon had 'hard-nosed business people ... eating out of his hands'. That is not easily done. To the surprise of some, Lord Sugar chose to hire Simon, even though he admitted it was a risky choice. 'Bloody old fool that I am, I'm going to take that risk. You're hired,' he told him.

Series four final task: Develop and market an original fragrance for men

In series four there were four candidates in the final. Alex and Helene formed the Renaissance team, the Alpha team comprised of Claire and Lee. In the previous week's interview round, Sugar had planned to fire three candidates but ended up firing just one. To their joy, the other candidates were all told they were going through to the final. Such was the quality of the candidates that year, Lord Sugar said he wanted to give all four one last chance to impress him.

The rival teams' fragrances each had strengths and weaknesses. Lee and Claire developed a scent called Roulette, which would be marketed at men who secretly aspired to be the next James Bond. The television advertisement they created for it reflected that theme. Nick Hewer was not impressed. 'For me Roulette equals gambling, equals debt, equals misery,' he said. Hewer was more impressed by Alex and Helene's fragrance, called Dual.

So did one of the expert industry panel who were called to give their assessments of the rival brands. Of Dual, he said: 'I may be the most quoted authority on perfume in the world. I might say, having nearly every product in the market sent into my office, considering you've had only had three days to make this I think it's extraordinary.' Unfortunately for Alex and Helene, Sugar felt the packaging was too expensive and for that reason they were the first to leave the final.

Which left Lee and Claire as the final two. Lee admitted he expected to finish second-best, but it was he who was hired by Sugar. 'When Sir Alan said the, "You're hired"cliché to me, it was unbelievable, fantastic,' he said. For many *Apprentice* viewers, the inclusion of four people in the final did not make for as satisfying or dramatic a showdown as did the traditional two-person final.

Series five final task: Create, brand and market a new box of chocolates

In series five, there were once again only two finalists: Kate and Yasmina. Kate's team chose to pitch their chocolate brand on a 'couples' theme. Their imagined slogan was 'for him, for her, to share' and they were originally planning to call the product Intimate. Then it was decided that this made it sound like a female sanitary product, so they changed the name to Choc d'amour. The expensive range included such flavours as strawberry & champagne, sea-salted caramel, passion fruit and honey & lemongrass.

Meanwhile, Yasmina developed a cut-price chocolate called Coco Electric. The packaging and business sense of her approach were admirable but it was felt that the chocolate product itself was of poor quality. Her flavours included strawberry & basil and chili & popping candy. Both candidates pitched their products and promotional campaigns to industry experts. Following all of that, Lord Sugar felt that Yasmina was the worthy winner of the series as she was daring, whereas Kate was robotic.

That said it was a close call. 'And these last two ladies, there is a gnat's whisker between them really, as far as

NICK HEWER AND
KARREN BRADY.

I'm concerned,' he had told Andrew Marr ahead of the final. 'Two very, very, very clever girls.' Indeed, Walsh claimed that Sugar had told her he had tried to change the rules of the *Apprentice* to allow him to hire her as well. 'Sir Alan phoned to say on Friday what the outcome was,' she said after the final. 'He said he tried to get the BBC to let him hire us both but he wasn't allowed because of the format of the show. It's a massive compliment and he said we were the best people he's ever had in the final.'

Series six: Create and launch a new alcoholic drink

More than in any previous series, the final of series six was one in which the choice of who was hired seemed informed largely by the performances at the final hurdle. 'This is your toughest task yet,' Lord Sugar warned the finalists at the start of the episode. Stella's team came up with a new brand of bourbon whisky that would appeal to female customers, while Chris came up with a pomegranate drink called Prism, packaged in a pyramid-shaped bottle.

Other suggested names for the drinks had been 'Young Heritage' for Stella's drink, but instead they went with 'Urbon'. Lord Sugar approved, saying: 'The name is good.' Though he wondered if the bottle made

KATE WALSH.

the product look more like vinegar. Chris lost control of his team, with two of his team-mates making the drink pink coloured even though they had been ordered to make it clear, so as to appeal to both males and females. His television advertisement was also inferior to Stella's, because he fussed too much over small details. To compound his misery, it was pointed out that his pyramid-shaped bottle might be unpopular among retailers, as it would take up a lot of room on the shelves.

These drawbacks meant that, although it was generally felt his drink tasted nicer than Stella's, he lost the task and then watched his rival crowned as the series winner. 'Do I want someone with more experience, or do I need the aggravation of training someone?' Lord Sugar had asked Chris. The outcome was that Stella was hired.

FRAUD

In January 2011, series six *Apprentice* candidate Christopher Farrell pleaded guilty to four counts of fraud by misrepresentation at Plymouth Crown Court. The mortgage broker was given a 9-month prison sentence, suspended for 2 years, and 200 hours' community service. The *Daily Star*, referring to the fact he had avoided jail, headlined its report: YOU'RE FREED! His arrest on fraud charges had been revealed on the eve of series six, at which time it was also revealed that he had two previous convictions for possessing an offensive weapon.

When the press discovered the skeletons in Farrell's cupboard it went hell-for-leather to try and dig up dirt on other candidates. The *Daily Mail* reported that candidate Joanna Riley had a brush with the law after a row with a taxi driver in Windsor. She pleaded guilty to 'causing racially aggravated fear or provocation of violence' for which she received a two-year conditional discharge.

It all made for some red faces in *Apprentice* circles. A *Daily Telegraph* journalist was coincidentally interviewing Lord Sugar the day that the fraud story broke in the *Sun*. According to the *Telegraph*'s report, the tycoon appeared to have tried to dissuade her from touching on the story, supposedly saying: 'I don't think you should devote too much space [in your article] to that ... Because it's the *Sun*. And it's not as serious as they're making out.'

Other reality shows such as *The X Factor* and *Big Brother* thrive on controversy and lurid tabloid stories about the lives of the contestants. It is a mark of the more dignified approach of *The Apprentice* that the

LORD SUGAR WITH WIFE ANN.

production team did not attempt to pursue the story further than it had gone already – a stance that has become the hallmark of many BBC takes on the reality-TV genre.

G is for...

GONGS

Since the first year it was broadcast, *The Apprentice* has won the hearts of the nation. It has also won plentiful awards, prizes and other gongs. These are official recognition of the excellence of the programme and the popularity it enjoys. Among the prestigious broadcasting awards that *The Apprentice* has won, are:

2005 Most Popular Reality Show at the National Television Awards.

2006 Best Feature at the BAFTAs★

2007 Features And Factual Entertainment Awards, Royal Television Society

2008 Best Reality at the TV Quick/TV Choice Awards

2009 Terrestrial Programme of the Year, Media Guardian Edinburgh International TV Festival

2009 Best factual entertainment at the 25th Broad-casting Press Guild (BPG) Awards.

GORGEOUS

Down the years, *The Apprentice* has featured contestants who are especially easy on the eye. Some of these stand-out as particularly fine-looking...

Series one: Sebastian Schrimpff

Series two: Michelle Dewberry

Series three: Kristina Grimes

★ When the series won the 2006 Best Feature BAFTA, Lord Sugar was amazed by the warm reception he received at the ceremony at the Great Room in the Grosvenor House Hotel. Throughout the evening he was approached by a string of enthusiastic television celebrities such as Jack Dee, Bruce Forsyth and Ricky Gervais. He was most excited to meet David Jason, whose television work he is an avid admirer of. Then he received the BAFTA from the evening's host Davina McCall. A nice night out, all in all.

JAMIE LESTER, CHRIS BATES AND JOANNA RILEY

CHARLIE BURDEN

Series four: Alex Wotherspoon
Series five: Kate Walsh
Series six: Jamie Lester/Joanna Riley

H is for...

HACKNEY

The London borough of Hackney has been the home of many famous people over the years. Among these are actress Barbara Windsor, gang leaders Ron and Reggie Kray and future Prime Minister of Britain Tony Blair. Lord Sugar was born in the borough too, within walking distance of the site of the Hackney Empire theatre. He has long supported the venue and has featured it on *The Apprentice*. In week five of series one, he set challenges to the candidates to negotiate with five celebrities for their services or property to sell in a charity auction, with the money going to the refurbishment of the theatre. 'The

CHARLIE BURDEN

Comic Tim Vine at the Sir Alan Sugar Challenge in the Hackney Empire.

restoration of Hackney Empire is a cause close to my heart,' he explained.

Watching the candidates interact with celebrities made for superb television. First Forte team member Raj became utterly star-struck in front of hypnotist Paul McKenna. He mumbled so badly that team leader James and Saira eventually had to step in and close the negotiation themselves. When the same team negotiated with comedian Mel Smith, they came away with just four theatre tickets as their prize. From Eamonn Holmes they procured a guided tour of the GMTV television studio.

Meanwhile, team Impact were doing much better with their celebrity meetings. Led from the front by Ben, the team thought big and used charm and humour to procure impressive prizes from the stars. Irish television personality Diarmuid Gavin gave them a Suzuki 600 motorbike and the cast of *Chicago* gave them 50 tickets to give away. Michael Winner chipped in with a dinner at The Ivy, but not before he had questioned the premise of the task. 'There are people starving, there are people dying, there is famine and drought,' he said. 'There are British people who cannot get into hospital. There is malnutrition and you are collecting for a variety theatre?' (Calm down, dear. It's only a television programme.)

They nearly blew their negotiation with feisty former Arsenal FC striker Ian Wright. Tim idolised Wright and this knocked him from his usual smooth-talking ways. Miriam stepped in and closed the deal. Afterwards, Campbell remained shaken. 'It knocked me,' said Tim. 'I'm not going to lie, it knocked me. It knocked me. I was knocked.' The auction at the Hackney Empire took an embarrassing turn when it appeared that nobody was going to bid for the four theatre tickets offered by Mel Smith. Fortunately, the evening's MC – and old friend of Smith-Griff Rhys Jones stepped in with a bid.

On the night the Impact team's superior prizes meant they won, by raising £18,000 to First Forte's £10,000. Central to their victory was the £6,000 that they secured for the Suzuki motorbike. Another factor that weighed things in their favour was that on the night of the auction they mingled with the crowd and drummed up plenty of enthusiasm for their prizes. Lord Sugar was made aware of this and he was impressed that they realised there was more to the task than just securing the best prizes. In the boardroom he decided to fire Sebastian, who he felt had made insufficient contribution. He called him a 'Cartier and Rolls Royce man', whereas Sugar described himself as a 'bang, bang, get things made' man.

Expanding on his decision afterwards, Lord Sugar gave a vivid insight into what he was after and – in reference to the fired candidate – what he was not seeking. 'Smoothy, smoothly, nicely, nicely, that's

GRIFF RHYS JONES AT THE SIR ALAN SUGAR CHALLENGE.

alright, but there's got to be a killer instinct somewhere and I don't think he's demonstrated it,' he said. It has been an entertaining episode and one that raised £18,000 for a cause close to Lord Sugar's heart. Good work all round, really.

In week one of series two, the candidates were sent to Spitalfields market to obtain fruit and vegetables to sell in Hackney. Velocity, the women's team, aimed to flirt their way to grabbing hold of as much over-ripe produce as possible. 'Our strategy should be free, free, free,' said Michelle Dewberry. It worked: they spent just £41 on produce while the male Invicta team spent £300 on theirs. The men's team's takings (£781) were dwarfed by that of the women's team (£1143) making Velocity the clear winners.

Even in victory, Velocity faced the wrath of Lord Sugar. One candidate had flirtatiously fed a grape to a passer-by to encourage a sale and Ruth had suggestively held a pair of melons in front of her chest. Velocity member Michelle Dewberry later defended this tactic, saying their strategy was misunderstood. 'Healthy Hackney, five portions of fruit and veg a day,' she called it. 'What better way to promote that than by fit young women in sports gear. Is that sex?' When it came to the firing, Lord Sugar sent Ben packing. He had been a poor, disorganised team leader, he was told.

AT THE CHARITY CHALLENGE HELD AT SUGAR'S BELOVED HACKNEY EMPIRE.

However, Sugar also gave Syed a stern warning that his card was marked.

Do not be surprised to see Hackney feature again in future instalments of *The Apprentice* and *Junior Apprentice*. Lord Sugar is proud of his connection to the area and many media types live nearby making it familiar terrain for many members of the production team. All in all it makes for happy hunting ground for the programme.

HOMESICKNESS

The Apprentice is not billed as a tough job interview for nothing. It is a rigorous and unforgiving experience that seeks to emulate the most testing aspects of the business world. It also isolates the candidates from their loved ones, meaning that homesickness becomes just one of the hurdles they have to be able to overcome to succeed and last in the competition. 'One of the first things that we tell them is, 'Look, you're gonna be away from home for twelve weeks,' Lord Sugar said when Ifti Chaudri complained in series three that he was performing below par because he was missing his family. In fact, though the show is broadcast over a 12-week period, the making of it is often condensed into just 7 or 8 weeks. Still, it is natural that some of the candidates will get homesick as they are confined into the bubble that is *The Apprentice* experience.

Ifti was a fine example of how even the toughest of contestants can fall prey to homesickness, particularly as his own circumstances at the start of the journey were so extreme. He was a former policeman and a black belt in martial arts, yet he found himself worried sick about his family during the first two rounds of series three. When Ifti left home to join *The Apprentice*, he had left a sick son and upset wife. At the end of the second task he admitted in the boardroom that his concern over this had been distracting him from the matter in hand.

Lord Sugar tried to be fair as well as firm. He told him he admired him as a 'good family man', but added that 'business is business, as you'll appreciate' and let him go. Ifti later explained the background to all this. 'When I left home my one-year-old son was pretty ill,' he told the *Manchester Evening News*. 'Leaving in that sort of circumstance was not a good thing. We were not allowed any type of contact. I felt that I was a little bit irresponsible not knowing what was happening. I just couldn't concentrate. I just gave up. It did hurt me intensely not knowing what could have happened.'

He told Digital Spy that the candidates are allowed no contact with their family during production: 'No, you're not. I can promise you one thing: if Sir Alan had said to me, "Just spend fifteen minutes with your son and check everything's OK," I could have gone on to the end. But you don't get any form of communication whatsoever. I think if I had been able to see my wife and check that my son was OK, I would have been fine.' The knowledge of the testing circumstances that the candidates are subjected to makes their performances on the series all the more admirable and their failings all the more understandable. This programme is no walk in the park.

Even winner Lee McQueen, who was notable for his alpha-male personality, admitted that he missed his girlfriend Nicola terribly during his successful *Apprentice* bid. 'Being away from Nicola for nearly three months was the hardest thing about being on *The Apprentice*,' he said. 'I just remember her running down the drive on the day I came home, throwing her arms around me and we both just burst into tears.' If the mega-butch McQueen can feel homesick, then anyone can.

In series five, one candidate lost his nerve before proceedings even got underway. On the opening episode, Lord Sugar told the assembled teams that one candidate had already 'bottled it' and left. The boss later explained to the press that the prospect of so long away from his family had made the candidate

dramatically reassess his plan. 'It was just that he got himself into his hotel room that night and realised that this is it, I'm away from up to twelve weeks from my family and my kids and I think the reality hit home,' he said.

The identity of the 'bottler' was kept secret on the programme. He was later revealed as Adam Freeman, a man who was clearly not short on bravado and confidence as he showed when he spoke to the *Sun* about his decision to quit. 'I knew I'd win it, so I would be away for twelve weeks,' he said. 'I did think about bailing out after a few weeks – but I would have looked like a bottler. I'm not a bottler. I work hard and always have done.'

Freeman also felt that his own similarities to Sugar – he is Jewish, left school at 16 and lives in Chigwell, Essex – might have worked against him. 'We would be like two peas from the same pod. Sir Alan would have been all over me like a rash. He would have wanted me to be as good as he's been all his life. I'm up for a bit of pressure, but he would have whipped me silly. And I knew I would have won it. It could have been hell. Let's face it – working for Sir Alan is no stroll in the park.'

So... he applied to take part in *The Apprentice* because he wanted to win it, but then left on the eve of filming because he was worried he would win it. It is a shame he did not decide to take part – with front like that he sounds like he would have been a very amusing candidate to watch.

I is for...

I DON'T LIKE...

When Lord Sugar originally met the candidates for the first episode of the first series of *The Apprentice*, he made a statement that would become part of the show's folklore. He was the only person who knew what he was going to tell the candidates. His first words were calm, mostly concerned with explaining how the process would work. Then he raised the stakes, warning them to never underestimate him and also informing them of some of his pet hates.

'I don't like liars, I don't like cheats,' he began, but there was more to come. 'I don't like bullshitters, I

ALAN SUGAR'S BELOVED HACKNEY EMPIRE.

don't like schmoozers, I don't like arse-lickers.' This became an iconic statement, immediately cementing *The Apprentice* and its anchor in the public mind. The impatient, threatening tone he delivered these lines in were so authentic that it elevated Sugar's position as far above that of the pantomime-dame 'baddy' of some other reality television shows. This was a business show and it was clear from the off that Sugar truly did mean business.

The fame this statement has acquired is by no means undeserving or unrepresentative. One of the most notable aspects of *The Apprentice* is the negative sense of much of the feedback and direction the candidates are given on screen. Lord Sugar spends more time saying what he isn't, what he doesn't want, than the opposites. 'I'm not going to tell you what to do, I'm going to tell you what not to do,' he said. The belligerent and critical tone this sets is what gives the show its drama. A programme fronted by a businessman hell-bent on finding a positive in every disaster or a good point in every dud candidate might feel a nice prospect. As a television show it would make for poor viewing.

Other famous lines from the business giant during opening sequences of various *Apprentice* series include:

'This is a business boot camp. Mary Poppins I am not.'

'The six-figure salary you'll win doesn't mean anything. I've been in business for forty years and your prize is working with me.'

'Don't start telling me that you're just like me, because no one's like me, I'm unique.'

'This is a job interview from hell. First prize, you get to work for me. Second prize, don't exist.'

'I've read all your CVs and on paper you all look good, but so does fish and chips.'

However, it remains the 'I don't like' list that Sugar and *The Apprentice* are most renowned for. It is regularly replayed on other television shows and has been parodied to comical effect. For instance, television presenter Paul Merton commented that it sounded like a grumpy man going through a restaurant menu at a bad restaurant. 'I don't like liars, I don't like cheats...'

INTERVIEWS

One of the most gruelling experiences that *The Apprentice* puts candidates through is left until near the end. The semi-final round sees the remaining candidates interviewed by trusted colleagues of Lord Sugar. However, the word 'interviewed' scarcely does justice to the intensive, ferocious grilling that they are given. These are conversations that often make the worst

Simon Cowell dressing-down seem tame in comparison. The entire series is billed as 'the job interview from hell', yet it is here that the candidates are literally put through a job interview – and they frequently find it hellish.

This is truly merciless stuff and the interviewers have become more brutal with each instalment of the series. For instance, in series four, property tycoon Paul Kelmsley informed Alex Wotherspoon: 'Your CV is one of the most boring CVs I've ever read.' In the same episode, former Amstrad trouble-shooter Claude Littner told Lucinda Ledgerwood: 'I've just been reading your CV and it looks to me as if, frankly, you are unemployable.'

However, Littner saved his real ire for his showdown with Wotherspoon, who he told: 'It's very unusual to find in your CV, someone that was born in England, actually puts down as one of his skills: English – fluent.' When Alex argued that he was doing very well in his career and much better than most people his age, Littner remained unimpressed. He snapped: 'Oh, do you have thick friends, then?' It had been a gruelling duel. 'He was an absolute bulldog,' said Wotherspoon afterwards.

In series five, Littner remained just as prickly. His soft and gentle voice somehow makes his harsh words carry

SERIES FOUR CONTESTANT LUCINDA LEDGERWOOD.

even more of a sinister tone. When candidate Paul Tulip told him: 'I'm just a likable person who can get along with anyone,' Littner replied: 'Well you're not getting along with me.' For many, Littner's finest hour came in series six when he interviewed Stuart Baggs (the brand). Baggs told Littner that he had applied for the series because he no longer wanted to be a big fish in a small pond. 'You're not a big fish,' Littner replied. 'You're *not* a big fish. You're not even a fish!'

Bordan Tkachuk is the chief executive of IT giant Viglen. He is also an infamous stickler for detail. More than any other *Apprentice* interviewer, he has unearthed some untruths on the CVs of applicants. He discovered the misleading information in the CVs of both Lee McQueen and Stuart Baggs. Having confronted them with what he discovered, he was unforgiving. 'What worries me is that here we have someone who is prepared to bullshit their way through,' he told McQueen. In series three he had Tre Azam on the ropes as he pointed out that the candidate knew next to nothing about Sugar's companies. Helmsley, too, showed he had done his research when he produced damning quotes from former tenants of Simon Ambrose. 'You should be embarrassed,' he told the quivering candidate.

For series six, former boardroom member Margaret Mountford joined the interview panel. She might not be a Rottweiler like some of the other interviewers, but she was not about to bring a soft touch to the party. Quizzing Jamie Lester on his response to the question on the application form 'What is the most interesting thing about you?', she quoted: 'I have a third nipple.' When Lester giggled nervously, she said: 'You're laughing, I'm not.' She then continued to plough through his application, and said: 'One or two pages later on – What's the worst lie you've ever told? "That I have a third nipple." Is that supposed to make me laugh? Think of a word that applies to that.' Lester stopped giggling and replied: 'Stupid.' He looked every inch the naughty schoolboy being told off by matron.

In previous years, Kelmsley had told one interviewee that the world of business is tough: 'People will cut your fucking legs off.' But the irony of the round is that, once the interviews are over, the quizzers are usually actually rather positive about the candidates. Having been rude to their faces, they are kind behind their backs as they report back to Lord Sugar on what they perceive each candidates virtues to be. They are two faced in an unconventional manner. When they leave the boardroom, they are replaced by the candidates for a bloodletting session that sees up to three of them fired.

The most notable post-interview firing came in series six. Stuart Baggs (the brand) had been ripped to pieces for the claims made in his CV about his online company in the Isle of Man. 'It's interesting that the regulator of the Isle of Man telecoms doesn't know anything about you,' said Lord Sugar. 'My guy is not a mug, he knows people. The thing is, my four advisers looked at me and said that you're full of shit, basically, and possibly you have been throughout the whole course of this process.'

He did not end his tirade there. 'What annoys me more is that, if I've misunderstood you with your claims, and everything else you said you've done, and someone like Liz left the process last week, I feel more sick. I don't believe a word you say, Stuart. I'm annoyed with myself.' That was the end of Stuart Baggs (the brand) – another contestant who was found severely wanting when interviewed.

The timing of the interview round, in the penultimate week of the process, is perfect. Candidates who have blustered or smoothed their way through previous tasks are suddenly given a rude awakening. There is no hiding place in the interviews round; this is a truly brutal experience. True, there is an element of pantomime about it. When the interviewing panel appear on the *You're Fired* show, it is clear that they are far warmer and kinder souls than they pretend to be during the main show.

But all the same, would you fancy your chances against any of them in a one-to-one encounter?

J is for...

JUNIOR APPRENTICE

It was Lord Sugar's idea to launch a junior version of *The Apprentice* – but the BBC needed some convincing. It took the persuasive master salesman over two years to convince the corporation that it was a good idea. He was working on a gut instinct that there were more young *Apprentice* fans than anyone had considered and that they would lap up an early evening, youth version of *The Apprentice*. Finally he persuaded the BBC to go ahead with the show, only to see it delayed when Lord Sugar's role in Gordon Brown's government prompted debate about the

LORD SUGAR AT A BUSINESS LAUNCH.

BBC's political impartiality regulations in the run-up to the 2010 general election.

Finally the show got the go-ahead to be broadcast in June 2010, though it would go out at 9pm, later than the slot originally envisaged by Lord Sugar. Over 28,000 youngsters applied to take part in the show. Ten candidates were selected, half boys and half girls, all aged either sixteen or seventeen. The prize at the end of the six-week contest was £25,000, which would go towards the winner's business career, personalised to their individual prospects and development.

The candidates were an impressive bunch of youngsters. Adam Eliaz was already running his own business and investing in stocks; Hannah Cherry was a budding inventor; Jordan De Courcy was running a successful online business; and Zoe Plummer was a creative all-rounder with excellent presence and organisational expertise. They were a kindly bunch, mostly lacking the high levels of backbiting and scheming that *Apprentice* candidates sometimes possess in droves.

Lord Sugar said that making the first series of the *Junior Apprentice* was the most fun of all the various series of the franchise. Alongside him were Nick Hewer and Margaret Mountford. The basic format was very similar to that of *The Apprentice*, but Lord Sugar was noticeably kinder to the candidates. Even when he fired candidates, he was careful to offer them positive feedback and encouragement for the future. The programme was definitely high on integrity.

Candidate Arjun Rajyagor confirmed that they were all given plentiful encouragement and praise from the board. 'Lord Sugar, Nick and Karren were all amazing role models and wonderful people to work around,' he said. 'They gave their criticisms and their praises but they were always fair. They always ensured that we all understood how much of an achievement it was that we had made it this far. They were always supportive and are still, to this day, people that I aspire to be like.' The lighter touch is palpable and heart warming. *Junior Apprentice* is a very welcome addition to the television calendar.

The final two were furry Lancastrian Tim Ankers – who had improved after a weak opening round in which he complained that 'wind is my least favourite weather type' – and geeky Essex boy Arjun Rajyagor. In an entertaining final, the four candidates were charged with the challenge of creating a branding and advertising campaign for bottled water. When it really mattered, Rajyagor shone brightest. Overcoming his reputation as just a 'numbers man', he showed creativity and poise at the final hurdle. Then, in the final boardroom of the series, he was articulate and confident, listing his achievements, including the computer-fixing business he ran from his bedroom and his head, prefect position at school.

It was a compelling case and was enough to tip the scales in his favour. Lord Sugar named him the winner of the inaugural series of *Junior Apprentice*. 'Arjun, I've spoken of your apparent soft nature, your clear academic qualifications,' he said. 'My concerns about you [are] adapting and trying to show that you can actually come up with that seed and spark of an idea that is needed in business.' He was willing to put his concerns to one side and name him the winner. 'Arjun has that natural business flair combined with intelligence that some people are born with – you can't learn it,' said an admiring Sugar. The winner described the moment of triumph as 'mind-blowing'. He said: 'Never in my wildest dreams did I believe that I would win when I first sent off that application form.' He added, 'But now that I have, I couldn't be more elated.'

It had been an entertaining and popular series, fully vindicating Lord Sugar's passionate backing of it as a concept. 'I've enjoyed *Junior Apprentice* tremendously – it was my brainchild,' he said. 'It was one reason for me continuing *The Apprentice*. The format's very good and the viewing figures keep growing, but there might

ARJUN RAJYAGOR WON THE TITLE OF JUNIOR APPRENTICE.

come a time when I think, I can't add to it. That's why *Junior Apprentice* came just at the right time and the BBC kind of detected that's how I felt about it – that I needed to do something else. The BBC are going to commission a longer series next time because six episodes wasn't enough.'

He added that *Junior Apprentice* candidates were a different breed. 'You don't have to be a brain surgeon to work out you need to work together,' he said, even though many *Apprentice* candidates failed at the hurdle. 'Refreshingly the junior apprentices are so fresh and green from school they've not got to that stage where they are their jostling for position, they are used to being told what to do, they get on with it and they are far more industrious.'

The second series of *Junior Apprentice* is scheduled for the autumn of 2011. Here's to plenty more series of it.

K is for...

KARREN BRADY

When Margaret Mountford stepped aside from *The Apprentice* at the end of series five, a replacement was needed. At the end of August 2009, it was announced that leading British businesswoman Karen Brady would be taking the vacancy. This was not the first time that Brady had been involved in *The Apprentice* – in series four and five she had appeared as one of the interviewers in the gruelling semi-final rounds. She had also been a team leader in the 2006 *Comic Relief Does The Apprentice*, leading her team to a romping victory and raising £750,000 for charity in the process. Lord

KARREN BRADY STEPPED INTO THE SIZEABLE SHOES LEFT BY
MARGARET MOUNTFORD.

Sugar was impressed, and Brady is in turn impressed by him and those like him. 'I love self-motivated, enthusiastic people,' she once said. 'Sir Philip Green and Lord Sugar are top of my list.'

However, Brady's qualification to join the series went far beyond those episodes. Often billed as 'the first lady of football', she worked at LBC Radio and Saatchi & Saatchi before conquering the beautiful game in 1993, when she became Managing Director of Birmingham City FC at the age of 23. During her 16-year reign at the Midlands club she turned its fortunes around. When she joined it had been a financially strapped club languishing in the lower reaches of the second division. By 2002 it was a profitable Premiership side. In January 2010 she moved to West Ham United FC as Vice Chairman.

Brady has also written several books, a column for the *Sun*, won countless business awards and is on the board of several charities and organisations including Scope and Channel 4. She has shown she is just as strong and driven away from work as she is in business. In 2009 doctors discovered a potentially lethal aneurysm on her brain. She underwent successful surgery and was back at her desk within a month. Just the sort of plucky spirit that Lord Sugar admires, had *The Apprentice* existed when she was starting up in business she would surely have romped home.

She had proved a wise choice to be one of the panellists during the interview round. She is a great reader of people and is clear about the four qualities she seeks in those she interviews. 'Firstly, that they have done their preparation – having done some background research on the company, who we are, where we are going etc,' she said. 'Secondly, that they understand and think about the job they are applying for; having a focus on exactly what they intend to bring to the role and the organisation as a whole. Thirdly, confidence. If they cannot sell themselves, they cannot sell my business. Finally, enthusiasm. I never employ anyone without this magic ingredient.'

Instead, she has joined it as one of Lord Sugar's trusted sidekicks. 'I love the show and it has been one of the best experiences of my life,' she said. One of the highlights of her involvement came in series six, as a fierce row erupted in the boardroom between the female candidates. 'You are representing businesswomen today, of which I am one, and some of your behaviour is outrageous,' said a disgusted Brady. 'You have to remember who you're representing in this process – young women out there who want to have an opportunity to do this. You should be an example to them.' Brady herself is certainly that. Lord Sugar had known her for 16 years when he chose her to join *The*

Apprentice as his sidekick. Though he admits they 'had some run-ins' in the past, he is a big admirer of this 'very shrewd lady'.

'Karren is different to Margaret. Margaret has her qualities and Karren has hers. She's not there to replicate what Margaret did, and certainly not to pull faces and do what she wouldn't usually do in real life.' As for Brady, she was blown away by the level of professionalism displayed by *The Apprentice* production team from the top to bottom of it. 'The amount of integrity and energy that goes into it is absolutely mind blowing,' she told *Glamour* magazine. Plenty of both of those qualities comes from the ever-impressive Brady.

KATIE HOPKINS

The Apprentice has produced many big personalities in its time, none more fascinating than series-three candidate Katie Hopkins. At the start of the show she described herself as a 'ruthless alpha female', but that was only the half of it. In fact, this former *Big Brother* applicant was a caustic self-publicist who stirred *The Apprentice* pot like no other candidate before or since. So loud was she that she fully merits her own entry, rather than being confined to the BIG MOUTHS section.

KATIE HOPKINS, SELF-CONFESSED 'RUTHLESS ALPHA FEMALE'.

Her notoriety was initially born out of her tendency to make rude remarks about fellow contestants. She said of Kristina Grimes: 'She does have a large mouth and I look forward to the day she tries to swallow something larger than she should. It will be the end of her.' Turning on her opponent's sense of style, she added: 'She is far too orange to be taken seriously,' and said. 'Whenever there's an issue, Kristina tries to cover her arse. It's a shame she doesn't do it a little better with the skirt she wears.' Ironically, she also damned Grimes as 'a hard little wench with a forked tongue'.

She snapped about fat people 'waddling to the boardroom', sneered at folk who watch television shopping channels and even people who had the temerity to be called Mavis or Derek. She poured particular scorn on Adam Hosker, making a direct insinuation about him in front of Sugar during a snappy boardroom session. She told Hosker: 'When your best friends are Mr Pinot and Mr Grigio you want to watch it.' On her application to the series, she wrote that she had lied 'to get someone else's husband because I wanted him' and she was photographed in the tabloids romping with a married man. During the show she was accused of having a fling with fellow contestant Paul Callaghan.

As a result of all this, she became a hate figure in the

press, finding herself compared to Cruella de Vil, Widow Twankey and Mis Piggy, among others. Even mild-mannered screenwriter Richard Curtis (responsible for such gems as *Notting Hill* and *Love, Actually*) joined in the bashing. During his acceptance speech for an award at the Baftas, he said his next ambition was to 'go out and kill that posh bird from *The Apprentice*'. Never before – or since – has the nation been so stirred up by an *Apprentice* candidate. This was national reaction of the sort of scale that is usually reserved for *Big Brother* baddies or *X Factor* phonies.

Even the nature of Hopkins' exit from the show was unconventional. She survived until the gruelling semi-final interviews round and was then offered a place in the final by Lord Sugar. He then noticed that she did not seem overjoyed. 'You don't look like a lady who's just been told you've entered the final,' he said. She replied that she was concerned about childcare arrangements and added: 'I don't want to make a fool of you or me. I think it's more important to get the courtesy to have my plans in place, so I'll have to stand down.'

With that, Hopkins was gone. She is therefore one of the few *Apprentice* candidates to hear neither 'You're hired' nor 'You're fired' from Lord Sugar. Since leaving the show she has carved out a career in the public eye, giving interviews to publications such as the *News of the World*, *Heat*, *Grazia* and appeared on countless television shows. She also took part in the 2007 series of *I'm a Celebrity... Get Me Out of Here!* and has sat on the panel on BBC1's *Question Time*, despite failing in her bid to become an MEP. Explaining her political aspirations, she said: 'I think it is time we had a straight talker, with a reputation for getting things done, speaking out for common sense. I am not well versed in the art of pleasing everyone like many "politicians" and I believe people deserve a straight and honest answer to a straight question.'

Final word on Hopkins goes to Lord Sugar, who was noble in his defence of her when interviewed on Jonathan Ross's chat show. 'Katie's been a tough cookie,' he said. 'There are loads of people like that in business, you don't have to love people, that's what the harsh commercial world is like and you have to put up with it.' At a time when few people were troubling themselves by seeking good qualities in Hopkins, it took the wise eyes of Britain's best-known businessman to pick them out. He is very fair and keenly wise. He had to be to be positive about Hopkins.

KOSHER CHICKENS

After the candidates in series four were sent to Morocco for their shopping task, Lord Sugar was so angry with their performances in the task that he threatened to sack all the contestants when they returned to the boardroom. It had been a colourful episode, one that threw many of the candidates far, far out of their comfort zones. The flashpoint of the episode came over one of the items on the shopping list – a kosher chicken.

This completely confused Jennifer, team leader of Renaissance, who said: 'Muslims have kosher meat.' She suggested that they buy a chicken and take it to a mosque to be blessed. Fortunately, at least one of her teammates could see the flaw in this plan. 'Am I being stupid or is kosher Jewish?' asked Claire. 'I don't think it's appropriate to take a chicken into a mosque.' They eventually purchased a chicken and asked the Muslim stallholder if he would bless it for them.

Back in the boardroom, Lord Sugar responded to all this with a mixture of fury, disbelief and amusement. It was Jenny's birthday as the boardroom scenes were shot, but Lord Sugar was not going to let that get between him and a good dressing-down. 'Are you telling me you don't know the term "kosher" is associated with Jewish people?' he asked her. She confirmed this was the case

MICHAEL SOPHOCLES WAS ALMOST AUTHOR OF HIS OWN CV TRAGEDY.

and Sugar got even more indignant. 'Is it right you went to a Muslim halal butcher and asked him to get you a kosher chicken – and he actually made a prayer over it?' he asked. 'Are you having a laugh or what? I don't know why you didn't go the whole hog and find a Roman Catholic priest to take the butcher to confession. It's unbelievable!'

As his anger soared, he was further incensed that the candidates were not co-operating with his investigations as much as he believed they should. 'If any of you are interested in staying in this process, you'd better start opening your mouth. I don't give a shit! I'll fire three of you! I'll fire all bloody five of you! Don't bother me at all!' he said. It is little wonder that Lord Sugar was stunned by their ignorance. One of the contestants, Michael Sophocles, had claimed to be 'a good Jewish boy' in his application to the series. When he was pressed on this in the boardroom, Sophocles came up with the evasive response that he was 'half-Jewish'. Sugar responded with a crude quip: 'If you're unsure you can always pull your trousers down and we can check.' (According to Jewish law, it is impossible to be half-Jewish.)

The hapless Sophocles eventually admitted that, though he did not know the meaning of the traditional Jewish toast 'L'chaim' (it means 'To life'), he was aware of the meaning of the word 'schmuck'. Which was just as well, because a nation of *Apprentice* viewers thought he was a prize example of one. There had been another culinary clerical cock-up in an earlier episode when the candidates found themselves trying to desperately offload some pork sausages. Just how desperately was revealed when Paul Callaghan observed: 'So, just to recap, we're trying to sell pork sausages to a Muslim and offering him a taster in the middle of Ramadan.'

P.S: In series six there was a touching moment when Jewish candidates Alex Epstein and Jamie Lester shared a celebratory hug at the very end of an episode. Lester crowned the moment beautifully by exclaiming: 'Kosher love.' In the same series, Melissa Cohen had boasted that she had 'single-handedly increased Tesco's share of the kosher food market to 75 per cent'. All in all, where series four was far from kosher, series six was as kosher as *The Apprentice* has been to date.

LORD SUGAR AND WIFE ANN.

L is for...

LONDON

The capital city of England, the scene of most of the series tasks, has almost become one of the characters of *The Apprentice* itself. It is to the capital that the candidates travel for the contest, and in the same city where much of the action takes place. 'Sixteen people have come to London in search of a job,' says the opening as it features them arriving in London by train, and walking along its streets and bridges as a group. The escalators at Waterloo and St Pancras stations have also been featured heavily in the opening rounds.

Special footage was also shot from above London

during specially commissioned helicopter rides. These sweeping scenes from the air take in the West End and also the financial district and Docklands area. The 'gherkin tower', Canary Wharf and other skyscrapers feature prominently. Such footage is cut in to the show to act as a stunning visual bridge between scenes. Watching all this glorious footage of the city is enough to make anyone fall in love with the place. London has never looked so good. This is footage as awe inspiring as aerial shots of Manhattan. 'I was very impressed when I first saw the sweeping views of London and the Thames,' wrote Lord Sugar of his first glimpse of the series.

The tasks have seen the candidates sell on London's street markets from the East End to the West End. They have also flogged pizzas on the South Bank, curated bus and walking tours to wow visiting tourists and dashed from shop to shop during the hectic, against-the-clock shopping tasks. During series six, Jamie Lester led a London bus tour in which he told puzzled tourists a series of 'facts'. 'On our left is the River Thames. It's the second largest river in London,' he said. As the bus pulled towards Westminster, he said: 'Straight ahead of you we've got Big Ben. The face of the clock is twenty diameters in width.' These were amusing moments, never to be repeated in a tour of London, one hopes.

THE LONDON SKYLINE
WITH CANARY WHARF
FEATURES PROMINENTLY
IN *THE APPRENTICE*.

During each series, the candidates live together in a grand London house throughout the process. The locations have included Chiswick, Hampstead, Notting Hill, Battersea and Ladbroke Grove. As a result of how London-centric *The Apprentice* is – its star being a man from east London – some viewers in the north of England have complained of a southern bias on the programme. This was a feeling fuelled by Jamie Lester's reluctance to take part in a task in Manchester, a city he felt is behind the times compared to London. 'I don't want to offend the Mancunians but they're always a step behind Londoners,' he said. 'You go to clubs in Manchester and you still have to wear shoes.'

There can be no doubt that the London of *The Apprentice* is a gleaming, thriving city. 'It used to be a pretty grungy place, but now it's really exciting again and we wanted to give it this celebratory aura,' explained director Andy Devonshire. In that aim they very much succeeded. Final word on the capital should go to adorable series-six star Alex Epstein. Whilst brainstorming for a name for a cleaning product, a colleague suggested 'Blitz', to which he replied: 'The Blitz was a big bombing thing, wasn't it, years ago, like the Blitz in London?' He eventually decided this was not a problem, adding: 'I think most people that were alive then are dead anyway.' And with that, the 76 consecutive nights of bombing that the Blitz constituted were swept aside.

When you are tired of London, you are tired of life, they say. How could anyone viewing *The Apprentice* tire of the capital city when it looks so great, vibrant and paved with opportunity? It is arguably as important a 'character' on the show as is Lord Sugar himself.

M is for...

MARGARET MOUNTFORD

When the first series of *The Apprentice* was being planned, it was agreed that Lord Sugar should have two sidekicks. Having convinced Nick Hewer to become one of them, Lord Sugar saw lawyer Margaret Mountford as the ideal candidate to complete a 'dream team' trio for the programme. He thought the idea of two well-spoken sidekicks, with himself as the 'rough diamond' in the middle, was irresistible. Little could he have known at that stage quite what a popular figure Mountford would become, as Britain fell in love with her withering on-screen ways.

MARGARET
MOUNTFORD
WITH NICK
HEWER.

Born in Northern Ireland in 1951, Mountford first met Sugar in the 1980s, when her law firm advised him during the flotation of Amstrad. As soon as he met her, he found her to be 'fiery... very serious and exact'. She then worked with him as he faced a legal battle with football manager Terry Venables over events at Tottenham Hotspur FC. 'That was exciting, but pretty horrible, too,' she recalled of the legal saga. 'The [Tottenham] fans were ghastly. You had to go past these awful spitting yobs on the way in and out of court, which is not what one is accustomed to as a City solicitor... Some fans, in my opinion, are little better than savages. It's very tribal.'

Throughout this work, she and Lord Sugar struck up a good understanding. Speaking of Lord Sugar, she amusingly said: 'He's a thoroughly decent bloke and he will listen' – here she inserted a dramatic pause – 'on occasions.' However, their mutual respect ran deep so it was to her that Sugar turned to suggest she became his sidekick. She was initially reluctant to join *The Apprentice*. Having always shied away from any publicity, she wondered why she would want to take part in a television programme that had every chance of becoming a big hit. However, Lord Sugar was convinced she would be the perfect lady for the job so he encouraged her to watch a video of the American

Apprentice, so she could see what was involved. She watched the video and, to Lord Sugar's pleasant surprise, told him she was up for the show. 'I accepted the invitation to do this because I thought it's something different,' she said.

What a hit she proved to be. With her silver hair, piercing blue eyes that she could roll to great effect, and possessing of a wonderful withering way with words, Mountford proved a shrewd choice. She became a cult hero among *Apprentice* viewers, who loved the way she filled the role of a stern headmistress, with a touch of the Judy Dench about her. It seemed nobody had a bad word to say about her. Nobody, that is, apart from Lord Sugar who told her during one episode that she 'couldn't sell a box of matches'. She explained later that she thought this was 'an unnecessary insult'. However, this was a mere blip in a relationship that continued to thrive on and off screen.

It was during series four of *The Apprentice* that Mountford's popularity soared higher than ever. When Michael Sophocles learned that his team's 'Singles' Day' greetings cards won a task, he celebrated like a deranged football fan, punching the air and yelling with excitement. Mountford's look of eyebrow-raised disdain was priceless. She had already behaved dismissively of Sophocles after watching his poor attempt at a Frank Sinatra impersonation during an Italian restaurant-themed task. 'I'm not sure what has more cheese in it, the pizza or that racket,' she said. Alex Wotherspoon also felt the force of her gently delivered sharp observational skills when he claimed that he had not 'stepped back' from the responsibility of becoming a team leader for a task. Mountford was having none of it. 'Alex, you stepped so far back from it you were practically out the room,' she told him. He dropped his head in shame.

Mountford's influence knew no bounds – she was crowned the 'Headmistress of the nation'. However, she makes for an unlikely and uncomfortable celebrity. She is normally bright and sharp, but admitted that the fame *The Apprentice* brought took her very much by surprise. 'I had no idea it would become so popular,' she said. 'I was very innocent about it really.' Soon she had to contend with being approached by strangers in the street. Her least favourite place to be recognised was while queuing at a supermarket checkout, 'when you have twenty-five minutes of queue ahead'.

In the summer of 2009 she announced that she would quit *The Apprentice* at the end of series five, so she could focus on her papyrology studies at UCL. 'I would like to concentrate on finishing this before I need a Zimmer frame to get on the platform to receive it,' she said. The public was heartbroken to learn of her departure, with *The Times* newspaper launching a 'Save Margaret' campaign. Nothing would persuade her to stay, though she did reappear in the interviews round of series six, where she quizzed the candidates.

She was just as entertaining and memorable as ever. When Stuart Baggs walked through the door for his interview, he greeted her as if they were long lost friends. 'Margaret!' he said with a big smile on his face. She did not reply in kind. Raising her famous eyebrows, she asked: 'Would you normally address an interviewer who you hadn't met by their first name?' Later in the interview, Baggs assured her he would work '24/7' if he were to be hired. 'And presumably you'd give it one hundred and ten per cent,' she asked.

The discussion got even more delicate when she challenged Jamie Lester over some attempts at humour on his CV. She was not amused by his declaration that he had a 'third nipple', declaring: 'You're laughing, I'm not.' And she was equally unimpressed one or two pages later to discover that his answer to the question: 'What's the worst lie you've ever told?' was 'That I have a third nipple.' Her withering response was: 'Is that supposed to make me laugh?' and with that, another male contestant was put expertly in his place by the headmistress of *The Apprentice*.

Throughout her years on the show, Mountford certainly made the viewers laugh. Her full-time presence on the show is sorely missed.

MARK BURNETT

It is surprising to learn that ants eating a carcass in a jungle was the inspiration for *The Apprentice*. Or is it? Some would say that is a perfect metaphor for what goes on in the tasks. Although *The Apprentice* franchise was born in America, its parent is from England. Mark Burnett is a titan of television, responsible for countless television hits of recent times. He was born in London in 1960, but raised in nearby Essex. He served for the British Army in Northern Ireland and the Falklands, receiving medals for his service in both territories. He then moved to America and became a 'nanny' in Beverly Hills, before peddling T-shirts on Venice Beach. He spent a lot of time closely observing American people, noting what made them tick. He entered the entertainment industry after selling footage to the ESPN television sport network of an adventure trek he had taken part in.

The first major television hit he enjoyed was with *Survivor*, which first appeared on American television in 2000. The high-octane reality show received six primetime Emmy nominations in 2001. He went on to create further reality-show hits, including *The Restaurant*, which appeared on the NBC network in 2003. The same year saw the first airing of *The Apprentice* on the same channel, a show created and

APPRENTICE CREATOR MARK BURNETT.

produced by Burnett. He had come up with the idea for it while working in the Amazon on *Survivor*. 'I saw a bunch of ants eating a carcass in the jungle and it reminded me of New York. You know, all these people crawling all over each other. Then I thought, what could I do in a place like New York? People need jobs; they need money. How about a televised job interview?' Having made a hit of *The Apprentice* in America he then sold it to England.

He continues to create and produce hits like *The Casino* and *The Contender*. Burnett was featured in *Time Magazine*'s 'Time 100 List' of the most influential people in the world and also named on the 'Top 101 Most Powerful People in Entertainment' list by *Entertainment Weekly* for the three consecutive years. What a success story. How *does* he do it? 'You try to tap into emotion,' he said. 'Social exclusion is a massive fear for people.'

When discussing his successful television career he has name-checked well-known philosophical giants including Joseph Campbell, Machiavelli and game theorist John Nash. A colleague said of Burnett: 'His brain never stops.' He also believes that the American spirit of never giving up is crucial to success. He recalls a story Donald Trump told him to illustrate how badly he suffered during the 1980s real-estate 'crash'. Trump saw a tramp on the street and thought: 'That guy is worth about $900 million more than I am at this minute.'

That Trump fought back from that low is, said Burnett, the spirit of *The Apprentice* and of his own life. The 21st century has seen many Brits become popular on American television, including Anne Robinson, Simon Cowell and Piers Morgan. Burnett shows that Brits are thriving behind the scenes just as much. In his spare time – yes, he does have some of that – he is a proper action man, a certified scuba diver and 'A'-level skydiver.

He is an impressive man: a decorated former soldier, award-winning television producer, bestselling author and multimillionaire. Mr Burnett, just one question: where did it all go wrong?

MERCHANDISING

Although *The Apprentice* has always been a modest reality show when compared to the rapacious, till-ringing commercial juggernaut that is *The X Factor*, it has spawned some merchandising. First to hit the shelves was a fine official book, entitled *The Apprentice: How To Get Hired Not Fired*. It was published by BBC Books in 2005, with an updated and revised edition

released the following year. It makes for entertaining and educational reading.

Readers were also wowed for a time by the official *Apprentice* magazine, which first appeared in 2007. As well as news from the show it also included features and nuggets of advice from captains of industry. A spin-off came in the shape of the chance to buy a personalised front cover, in which your name would be included in the headline announcing the winner of *The Apprentice*.

Generally considered the finest official *Apprentice* merchandising was the podcast, hosted by former Blue Peter presenter Richard Bacon. Nicknamed 'The Apprenticast', it included interviews with fired candidates, as well as hilarious, irreverent commentary galore. Bacon did not always call it right during the podcast. In series three he said it was 'obvious' that Sugar did not want eventual winner Simon Ambrose to win.

Fremantle Media Enterprises was behind the podcast, along with production company Somethin' Else. Bacon has continued to be a celebrity fan of *The Apprentice* and occasionally has former candidates, including Raef Bjayou, on his Radio 5 Live Evening programme. His podcast is sorely missed by those who followed it. However, *Apprentice* fans who enjoy a bit of iTunes action can also, as of April 2009, download episodes of the series to watch at their leisure.

N is for...

NICK HEWER

Since he first worked for Lord Sugar in 1983, Nick Hewer has proved a valuable sounding board for his boss. Add to the mix that he is a public-relations genius who knows inside out how the media works, and he became the ideal candidate to join the *Apprentice* board. His semi-military character makes for entertaining viewing. Although he is not as fond of extravagant, dramatic facial gestures as Margaret Mountford, he has wonderful winces and idyllic eye-rolls in his locker.

Born in Swindon, Hewer was schooled by Jesuit priests in County Kildare at an establishment James

NICK HEWER.

Joyce wrote about in his novel *A Portrait of the Artist as a Young Man*. When he left that establishment his father handed him a five-pound note and told him to go and 'make it' on his own. He did. He studied law for a while but it was public relations that he was going to make a living in. He worked alongside Sugar in a number of projects including Amstrad ventures, his ill-fated football reign and a number of personal ventures.

By Lord Sugar's admission, he has often proved a frustrating client for Hewer to work with. As a man not keen on publicity and certainly not keen on granting interviews, he caused his PR man to 'tear his hair out' with frustration. So there is an irony in the fact that, when it came to *The Apprentice*, it was Sugar that had to persuade Hewer to take on a media gig. As Hewer put it: 'I fought against it, and Alan got really irritated as only he can, and he said, "Of course, if you don't think you can do it..."'

Hewer said that Sugar got 'very shirty' about it and he eventually relented and signed up to the show. He is the perfect man for the job of hovering in the background as the candidates undertake each task. With his neatly cropped silver hair and sharp, wise eyes, he is the ultimate observer. He takes copious notes throughout the process and delivers razor-sharp reports to Lord Sugar. In addition to this role, he also delivers witty on-the-spot comments. 'I wouldn't feed that food to Margaret's cat,' he once said of a food product an *Apprentice* team had come up with.

Although his charm lies more in facial expressions and generally exasperated demeanour than it does in classic lines, he has delivered plenty of bon mots. 'You were all over it like a tramp on chips,' he once told a team after they enthusiastically took on a concept after a focus-group meeting. He memorably described the controversial Katie Hopkins as a 'silly girl', adding: 'She was kind of five degrees off normal, wasn't she? Extraordinary.' However, he has respect for what all the candidates go through during the process. 'I found it tiring just watching them,' he said after series one. 'Heaven knows what they must feel.' He particularly feels for any candidate who faces the wrath of Sugar in the boardroom. 'People have been reduced to nervous wrecks,' he said. 'Sugar's got this twenty-second black stare, where his pupils appear to completely dilate and they go right through you and he's just silent. It's very unnerving.'

He is a compassionate, observant man. In fact, the on-screen perception that there is a fair distance between the candidates and the board members is not entirely accurate of the wider picture. During the tasks, Mountford and Hewer had often eaten with the candidates during tasks, chatting away as they would in any circumstances. Brady insists there is suitable distance, though. 'Nick and I are very conscious to keep our distance really,' she said. 'We're not their friends, we're not their mentors, we're not their advisor. Our job is purely to observe and watch what they do so we can give an accurate report. We don't fraternise.'

Hewer, a man who had previously stood in the background, has become a public figure thanks to his involvement on the show, though he insists that he does not 'hang around Oxford Circus' trying to be recognised. Likewise, when people try and get him to spill details about a forthcoming series or episode, he bats them away, telling them: 'The BBC implants a small explosive device in us and if we say the wrong thing our heads blow up.'

His friendship with Lord Sugar is now in its fourth decade. He attended the 40th wedding anniversary of his boss and gave a witty speech that had guests rolling with laughter. Lord Sugar later wrote that Hewer 'might have had rather a lot of the superb red wine'. Describing Hewer as 'one of his most trusted colleagues', he has chosen well. When *The Apprentice* production team agreed to put this at first unlikely man on screen, they, too, chose wisely. *The Apprentice* would be considerably weaker without him.

O is for...

OPENING LINES

The opening episode of each series of *The Apprentice* is notable for the passionate statements made by each candidate in their introductory videos. This is the first glimpse the viewers get of the candidates who will become like personal friends in the coming weeks. While the candidates attempt to exude confidence and gravitas, they often exude rather toe-curling babble. They are pumped up and puffed up to the hilt, preening themselves as they compete to make the most dramatic and self-aggrandising statement. Far

JENNIFER MAGUIRE (LEFT, WITH JENNY CELERIER): 'I CAN SELL PIECES OF PAPER ON THE STREET FOR £50.'

from impressing the viewers, they often provoke only amusement and scorn from those watching them.

Often, the more silly the remarks, the more entertaining they are. So here are some high/lowlights:

Shibby Robati: 'My first word wasn't Mummy, it was money.'

Ben Clarke: 'To me, making money is better than sex... it's that rush.'

Ian Stringer: 'In life there are two types of people. There are winners... and the second one... I can't say it, I won't say it.'

Michael Sophocles: 'I am quite happy to cut people out of my life if I think it's going to help me be a success, be a winner.'

Ifti Chaudhri: 'When you can break bricks with your bare hands, you believe in your head that you can do anything.'

Tim Campbell: 'Sir Alan has a lot he could teach me. Perhaps I might know a few things that I could teach him as well.'

Jenny Maguire: 'I can sell pieces of paper on the street for £50.'

Stuart Baggs: 'I am Stuart Baggs, The Brand... everything I touch turns to sold.'

Mona Lewis: 'I knew I would be selected, not to sound big headed...'

Paloma Vivanco: 'I'm a hyper-achiever. Everything I do is always a success.'

Of all the boastful phrases that he has heard, Lord Sugar said that one has stood out as particularly objectionable. 'It's the cliches really – "I think outside the box". I think there's a kind of drone that you ignore. I have this ability to switch off when they start talking like that,' he said. Future applicants – take note!

P is for...

POLITICS

In 2009, *The Apprentice* got caught up in the world of party politics when Lord Sugar became a Labour peer. In the wake of this development, a complaint was lodged by shadow culture secretary Jeremy Hunt claiming that Sugar's government role as a Labour peer conflicted with his BBC work on *The Apprentice* as the country prepared for a general election. The BBC Trust's editorial standards committee explored the complaint and ruled that the 'combination of Sir Alan's roles as star of a BBC entertainment show, government adviser and peer and the proximity of the next general

LORD SUGAR ARRIVES FOR A MEETING WITH PRIME MINISTER GORDON BROWN IN DOWNING STREET.

election poses a greater than normal risk to the impartiality, integrity and independence of the BBC in relation to the broadcasting of *The Apprentice* and *Junior Apprentice* next year'.

The ruling was an unflinching, heavily phrased affair. It also said the BBC faced a 'particular risk' with Sugar because, 'in the public's eye, Sir Alan [sic] is now both an iconic figure, a key part of the BBC brand as star of *The Apprentice*, but he is also a political figure with two political roles as government adviser and Labour peer'. The ruling continued: 'The risk that the BBC's impartiality, integrity and independence will be compromised and/or public confidence in the BBC will be undermined is therefore greater in respect of Sir Alan Sugar than for other comparable BBC on-air talent.' This was not a report that left much room for doubt.

For this reason, series six of the show (and series one of *Junior Apprentice*) did not appear in its usual springtime slot. Instead, both shows had to wait until after the general election in May 2010. Only once that election had come and gone did the two programmes get shown. With *Junior Apprentice* beginning first, the sixth series of the main show did not begin its run until deep into autumn. This meant that nearly a year had elapsed between the filming of series six and its broadcast. Sugar was not happy. Having frequently taken risks and stood up to authority throughout his business career, he was frustrated that the corporation had not been more sturdy. 'Everybody was disappointed that it got delayed,' he said. 'It was a big political thing and the BBC lost their nerve, simple as that.'

As his fury grew, he also wondered whether there was a double standard at work. Why was musical man Lord Andrew Lloyd Webber allowed to continue appearing on the BBC talent search *Over the Rainbow* despite his own political preferences being well known? 'We saw him in The *Sun* newspaper last week saying he backs Mr Cameron,' noted Lord Sugar. The BBC insisted that there was a significant difference between expressing political opinions and stating preferences. Of Lord Lloyd-Webber, the BBC said: 'We advise prominent figures working with us to avoid intervening in the political debate at times like this. However, he is at liberty to express his opinions, which he has made no secret of in the past.'

Yet Sugar's peerage undoubtedly crowned a lifetime of achievements – one that had not exactly been short of honours before. When Alan Sugar became Sir Alan Sugar in 2000, it was a knighthood that came for services to business. It was an amazing day for the man from Hackney as he arrived at Buckingham Palace. It

THE SUGARS ON A TRIP TO
CLARIDGES HOTEL, LONDON.

was, he said, 'one of the proudest moments of my life'. However, when it was announced nine years later that he was to become Baron Sugar, of Clapton, in the London Borough of Hackney, there was nevertheless controversy galore. Some commentators described the move as a publicity stunt.

Lord Sugar is such a success story and fascinating character the he has inevitably been admired by politicians of all colours and hues for years. Lord Young, who was Secretary of State for Trade and Industry under Margaret Thatcher's premiership, said: 'He's one of a new breed of British entrepreneurs. I would like to see people like that as role models for young people coming into business. I want people to say, "Damn it, if he can do it, I can."' Not that Sugar is a Conservative, even though he naturally appealed to their 'enterprise culture'. He spotted the need for a New Labour years before it came about. In 1990, he said of Labour's prospects of retaining power: 'The Left cannot be as our fathers would remember it in the old days. If the Labour Government comes in, their policies will have to be virtually the same.'

Soon after his peerage, he gave an interview to the BBC's *Andrew Marr Show*. When he arrived in the studio, he was greeted by newspaper journalist and broadcaster Andrew Neil, who made a joke about

Sugar's appointment being a case of 'a rat joining a sinking ship'. Lord Sugar gave as good as he got, also warning Neil that he could tell the viewers 'a few stories about you' when he went on air. It was not a promising start. Sugar was in no mood to be messed with and the presenter, Andrew Marr, would realise this during their live, on-air exchange. He asked Lord Sugar if he felt there was conflict of interest between his political appointment and work on *The Apprentice*.

Lord Sugar began his answer by pointing out that *The Apprentice* is not about politics, but about 'buying too many chickens or not selling enough flowers'. He then let rip with a verbal onslaught that was as fearsome as anything he had unleashed in *The Apprentice* boardroom. He told Marr that *The Andrew Marr Show* is 'the biggest reality TV show on air'. Explaining his thesis, he said: 'What you do is interrogate people like myself and Gordon Brown and Peter Mandelson...You don't really care who we are; we're just contestants – it's a game for you.' Marr had taken part in many a feisty interview in his time, but this was superbly spiky stuff.

Sugar was not in a mood to stop. He added that even if the Conservatives won the next general election, nothing would change. 'We are nothing to you other than good TV, part of the biggest reality show on earth. Both you and that tubby fellow from

Sky, Adam Boulton, stand outside Number Ten and abuse Gordon Brown. Then there's that ginger bird, Kay Burley... it's all part of a big charade, Andrew. In fact, what you do is no different to me hosting *The Apprentice.*' It didn't really address the point, but it made for gobsmacking television. A Sunday-morning mini-episode of *The Apprentice*. Indeed, the only thing lacking from his titanic tantrum was the crowning line: 'Andrew, you're fired!'

Even when Lord Sugar took his place in the House of Lords chamber for the first time, *The Apprentice* featured. He told his fellow peers that he was aware some sceptics had awarded him the status of 'the telly peer'. 'Well, my Lords, with that in mind, those of your lordships who may have stumbled upon the TV show may recall when it started six years ago I made the statement, "never, ever underestimate me".' That was the only direct quote from the show that he made in the speech, but there were other moments in it that came from the same place.

'I'm straight, I'm blunt and I won't always be popular,' he told the Chamber. 'But I promise you this. I will always be honest, and passionate about assisting SMEs and getting our young people to think about business as an opportunity.' He left the chamber when Lord Oakeshott of the Liberal Democrats rose to speak.

Oakeshott had recently apologised to Lord Sugar for claims he had made about him after his appointment. He had said Lord Sugar might not be a 'fit and proper person' to sit in the Lords. However, he was about to speak out again against his peerage, and would use *The Apprentice* as a stick to beat him with as he did so.

'Noble Lords may not realise that he is one of our most successful property tycoons, with net assets estimated at £730 million in this year's *Estates Gazette* rich list,' said Oakeshott of Sugar. 'The Amsprop Estates website displays a fabulous selection of prime West End properties from Bond Street to Park Lane, so if the noble Lord ever gets bored with starring in *The Apprentice* I am sure that he would be equally brilliant in *Location, Location, Location*.' Even as he stood in the House of Lords, Lord Sugar could not escape the ever-present influence of *The Apprentice*. He must have wished he could point his finger at Oakeshott and say: 'You're fired.'

Other instances where *The Apprentice* has crossed over into the world of Westminster and the wider political landscape include the time in 2005 when then Chancellor Gordon Brown announced plans for special business camps for teenagers. Mr Brown came up with the idea for the camps after watching *The Apprentice* and also hearing Sugar speak to a group of teenagers in his trademark robust style. Some *Apprentice* alumni have attempted to build careers in politics, including Katie Hopkins. Karren Brady is interested in the field herself, though she stops short of aiming for the top job. 'I like politics and would like to be an advisor in a political arena, but my ambitions don't extend to being the PM,' she said.

PONY

A regular *Apprentice* hobby horse is the question of whether a candidate is a 'one-trick pony'. It is typical of the ferocity of the process that as soon as a candidate is shown to excel in one skill area (selling, presentation, strategy etc.) that rather than being praised for it, they are made to face the accusation that they only have that one skill. So it was that in series two, a badger got accused of being a pony. 'Are you just a one-trick pony?' asked Lord Sugar of stunning Brummie saleswoman Ruth Badger. 'A one-trick pony?' she responded later. 'I'm one hell of a pony and I know a lot of people would put a lot of money on me!'

The pride of the *Apprentice* pony accusations came in series six when Stuart Baggs (the brand) was facing elimination. With his back against the wall he came out fighting and made an impassioned boardroom speech

RUTH BADGER – NOT A ONE-TRICK PONY.

that was unprecedented in *Apprentice* annals. He spoke with enthusiasm aplenty in an outburst that veered between the touchingly poignant and the cry-with-laughter ridiculous.

After listening with a mixture of smirks and sighs, Lord Sugar finally intervened to point out that the candidate was making 'outrageous promises'. This only spurred the young man to ever greater and more astonishing vows. 'I'm not a one-trick pony, I'm not a ten-trick pony,' he said with passion in his eyes. 'I've got a field of ponies and they are waiting to literally run towards this.' While the other candidates struggled to contain their mirth, Lord Sugar told Baggs he would one day look back on his speech 'and cringe'.

One imaginative online store has produced a range of 'Field of ponies' T-shirts to commemorate Baggs' boast. Baggs is a long, long way away from the day when he can finally live down his pony moment.

POSHOS

The Apprentice has attracted contestants from all backgrounds. Some of the most memorable have been the well-spoken posh candidates. Here are the cream of the upper-class crop...

James Max

Educated at St Paul's School, James Max obtained a first-class BSc in Land Management and then worked as a chartered surveyor, including a stint alongside rugby star Rob Andrew. Among the firms he worked for were Morgan Stanley. This pedigree placed him at the top of the social ladder for series one of *The Apprentice*.

He had a smooth personality and presence, with the air of a serial diplomat. Time after time he was on the winning team, including in week four when he led Impact to victory in the Harrods task. Their reward seemed thoroughly fitting for a team led by such a well-bred man: a helicopter trip around English stately homes. He tasted defeat as project manager in week seven, but survived the chop in the boardroom showdown. Three weeks later he was project manager again and steered his team to another win in the teleshopping task.

However, he left after the gruelling semi-final when the interviewing panel doubted whether he was truly intent on working for Amstrad. Since leaving the show he has pursued a career in the media. His posh dulcet tones have been broadcast over the airwaves by such radio stations as TalkSport and LBC. He has also appeared on television shows and taken on some corporate gigs. For his part, Lord Sugar did not run *The Apprentice* to help candidates launch a bid for celebrity. In the future he would

RAEF BJAYJOU WITH FELLOW CONTESTANT ALEX WOTHERSPOON.

watch out for candidates such as Max. When he learned that a contestant was planning to do a naked photo-shoot if he won, Lord Sugar reportedly issued a ban on such a move. 'He thinks it puts a black mark

against his name,' said a source. 'Anyone working for him has to be dedicated to the job, not, as he puts it, fannying around in the media. Sir Alan may search for an apprentice on a TV show but that doesn't mean he endorses celebrity behaviour.' The shadow of James Max lived on.

Raef Bjayjou

Raef Byajou was the definitive posho of series four. Having been educated at two fine independent schools in Hertfordshire one of which made him school captain, he then studied History and Politics at Exeter University, where he became a committee member of the debating society. He is a keen lawn-tennis player. After graduation he began his entrepreneurial career with an irrigation company in Ethiopia before deciding, understandably, that entering *The Apprentice* might be more fun.

With his upright, athletic stance, his dapper way with clothes, and his clipped, well-spoken voice, he was a stand-out contestant throughout his *Apprentice* journey. On the opening episode, he said: 'The spoken word is my tool' and was quickly described as 'splendidly dotty' by the *Daily Mail*. He later agreed that such an assessment was accurate, particularly given the way the editing of the show had presented him as 'a ridiculously pompous pillock instead of the affable and gregarious person that I am'.

Since leaving *The Apprentice* he has become a minor television celebrity, appearing on Living TV's *The Underdog Show*, Channel 4's *Come Dine With Me* and *Celebrity Coach Trip*. Throughout all these appearances he has remained his usual classy and cultured self. He has also inherited his uncle's £6.5 million Mayfair apartment. Lord Sugar described Byajou as 'really nice chap'. He did indeed seem a 'bloody good bloke'.

Other, minor, *Apprentice* poshos include the extravagantly named Nicholas de Lacy-Brown, a trainee barrister who was educated at King's College London. He was facing an almost certain firing in week one of series four and in attempting to save his backside told Sugar: 'I'm very into art and culture and that sort of thing... I find it very difficult to have conversations about football, for example.' Hardly words to endear him to the former Tottenham Hotspur chairman from Hackney. Another briefly featuring posho was Raleigh Addington, the well-spoken Exeter University graduate who left after one week of series six after his soldier brother was injured in Afghanistan. Raleigh will be most remembered for his 'It was shameful!' outburst in the boardroom in week one, as the men's team's failure was discussed.

APPRENTICES MICHAEL SOPHOCLES AND LINDI MNGAZA

PRAISE

The Apprentice truly hit the ground running when it was launched. It immediately prompted much pride and self-praise from the great and the good of the BBC. 'In a very short space of time, it has become one of the most talked-about shows on television and the feedback from the audience has been fantastic,' said Roly Keating, controller of BBC Two. Jane Lush, controller of entertainment commissioning at the BBC, added: 'I'm thrilled that this mix of business and entertainment has captured the imagination of the audience who would never normally choose a programme centred around the skills of business – water-cooler TV at its best.'

The praise was soon raining down from outside, as well. *The Apprentice* crossed all boundaries, with tabloids and broadsheets alike loving every minute of it. The *Sun* said the series was 'The thinking man's reality show', while The *Mirror* described it as 'jaw-dropping viewing'. Meanwhile, the London *Evening Standard*'s verdict was that *The Apprentice* is 'terribly compelling'. Over in the land of the broadsheet, *The Sunday Times* crucially saw it as a genuine business programme: 'This is not just a game show: it's a business school.' The *Daily Telegraph* described *The Apprentice* as 'the most addictive show in years', and The *Guardian* decided that it

Contestant Debra Barr.

provided 'a salutary lesson in aggressive buying and selling, hiring and firing'.

'It's a great format, it's beautifully shot, it's well edited and at the centre of it, there's a brilliant figure in Sugar,' said Ally Ross, the influential TV critic for The *Sun* newspaper. 'There's a reasonably engaging set of maniac characters cast as well. It's certainly a lot more realistic than, say, *Big Brother*. In essence there's realism to *The Apprentice*. It's a bit of a contrived situation, but that's what gives it the edge over other reality shows.' The fact that newspapers from across the cultural and social spectrum so heartily approved of the series showed how broad its appeal was from the very start.

Perhaps the most satisfying praise of all came from The *Independent* newspaper. *The Apprentice* was launched relatively late on in the reality-television era. There was therefore a danger that it would be dismissed as a reality show too far. However, The *Independent* concluded quite the opposite. 'There is a feeling among reality-TV experts that *The Apprentice* may be the best programme of its genre ever shown on British television,' it chirped. 'It has all the trappings of core reality programming: a group of ordinary people who want something and are tested on television to get it.'

Q is for...

QUALIFICATIONS

Lord Sugar is not one to be impressed by university degrees or other educational certificates. 'Qualifications are meaningless in the world of business,' he said. 'They are a badge that shows a person is at a certain level of intelligence – it doesn't demonstrate that they are an expert in anything.'

QUOTABLES

Throughout the pages of this book there are plenty of memorable quotes from *The Apprentice*. With the candidates under such immense pressure and scrutiny for so long, it is inevitable that they will come out with quotable lines. The morning after many episodes, viewers enthusiastically repeat the latest quotes to one another. But some candidates are more quotable than others. Here is a selection of *Apprentice* stars who have produced particularly funny one-liners.

Melissa Cohen

On rival Joanne Riley: 'I find it very difficult to conversate with her.'

On her fellow candidates, after she had been fired: 'Karmically, they will be retributed.'

During a tense negotiation on prices: 'There's no room for manoevrement.'

Stuart Baggs

'I am Stuart Baggs, The Brand.'

'Everything I touch turns to sold.'

'Come on, ladies and Gentlemen, fancy a taste of my jellied eels?'

'I'm not a cliché.'

'Excuse me, sir, you look like a sausage connoisseur.'

'What's £100,000? That's about £65,000 after tax. I wanted way more. I wouldn't get out of bed for that.'

The quotable Stuart Baggs.

Claire Young

'I hate snakes. If Sir Alan, for a million pounds, came up to me and said, "Claire, kiss that snake," I'd say, "I'm sorry. I'd rather kiss you!"'

Raef Bjayou

'I think that we need to remember that those in a size 16–32 dress, are size 16–32 for a reason: they love cake.'

Ben Clarke

'I would say Kim, clinically speaking would be considered obese. And James isn't obese, but you can tell he's not exactly fit. He could do with going for a few runs.'

Lucinda Ledgerwood

'Stop it! Not on! Naughty, Naughty, Naughty!'

James McQuillan

'I feel like a monkey learning to use tools.'

'The mother needs to be happy because if she's a bit anxious there's something in nature that switches off the tap in her breast.'

(During a video shoot with two gay male actors): 'Not so much of the suggestive licking, we're not shooting a porno.'

CLAIRE YOUNG OUT WITH FRIENDS.

R is for...

REWARDS

In *The Apprentice*, the winning team always gets a prize for their win – to the victors, the spoils, as they say. At the end of each task (excluding the semi-final and final) the winning team is told by Lord Sugar that they will receive a 'reward' for their victory. Having fought and worked so hard to seal the win, the candidates are often drained and therefore especially welcome a treat. For the viewers, there is something rather tickling about watching grown adults being told they are to receive a 'reward'. It is reminiscent of a child being told he is allowed a special treat.

The first ever reward, at the end of the first task of series one, was a trip to the London Eye. It was enjoyed by Impact team leader Tim, who eventually became the series winner and the first ever apprentice. Later rewards in series one included a clay-pigeon shooting session at a country club, a trip to Monaco with the proceeds of the relevant task provided to gamble and a relaxing pampered stay at a Scottish castle. All of which are experiences far preferable to a slap in the face or a cup of tea in the Bridge End Cafe.

The rewards in series two were an even more exciting mix. From the trip to the Royal Ballet in week one, to a luxury meal at The Dorchester in Mayfair, a pampering session at a leading spa, indoor sky-diving in a wind tunnel and a racing-car driving day at the Bedford Autodrome, it was a good year to be on the winning teams. In subsequent series the familiar mixture of culinary, pampering and action-packed rewards continued. New themes were introduced, such a private piano recital from musician Myleene Klass in series four and a private performance from soprano Katherine Jenkins. There have also been a yoga and laughter-therapy session and a caricature provided for each member of a winning team by cartoonist Gerald Scarfe. The most prized rewards of series six were a weekend trip to Paris and a spending spree at the stores of top fashion designers.

MYLEENE KLASS – HERE WITH KARREN BRADY – GUESTED ON
THE APPRENTICE.

On occasions, a candidate on the losing team has had extra reason to be envious and despairing when they realise what reward they have missed out on that week. Never was this more the case than when Adam Hosker missed the speedway reward that followed the task he was fired for. To try and make up for his palpable heartache, he was presented with some tickets to a speedway track during his appearance on the official *Apprentice* podcast. In series six, too, there was a motorsport-themed reward when a winning team visited Brands Hatch, to drive M3 Master cars.

S is for...

SANDHURST

Poor Ben Clarke: he thought his oft-repeated line that he was once offered a scholarship at the Royal Military Academy at Sandhurst would make him stand out from the pack in a good way. Instead, it made the Gavin Henson lookalike stand out in a terrible way as fellow candidates, board members and viewers alike became exasperated by his regular citation of this fact, not least because he had never taken up the offer.

The Daily Telegraph concluded: 'History records few evil Bens. We've never had a Ben the Hun or a Ben the Terrible or a Ben Hitler. Not even a Benghis Khan. But

BEN CLARKE, SANDHURST APPRENTICE.

the current series of BBC One's reality show *The Apprentice* has changed all that. A mere four episodes into the run, Ben Clarke, the shrilly self-promoting contestant from Belfast, is establishing himself as the most reviled man in the country outside the Cabinet.' It may seem harsh, and it is, but Clarke did himself no favours by obsessively prattling on and on (and on and on) about Sandhurst.

Finally, people began to challenge the hedgehog-faced Clarke when he reminded them about his Sandhurst offer. As he repeated it for the umpteenth time during a car journey, fellow candidate Philip Taylor asked him: 'Did you go?' to which an instantly deflated Clarke could only reply: 'No.' Then, Lord Sugar's patience snapped in the boardroom. 'Don't start banging on about bloody Sandhurst again,' he told him. 'I was in the Jewish Lad's Brigade, Stamford Hill Division, but it didn't make me sell computers when I got older!'

Nothing could take the wind out of Clarke's sails for long. In case you hadn't guessed, he was not a candidate one could describe as lacking in confidence. 'It makes perfect sense that I do the modelling,' he said one week. 'Out of the men, I'd say I probably am the best looking.' He was a master of the boardroom showdown, with his amazing knack of saying: 'Can I just finish?' the moment he thought another candidate was getting the better of him. Even before such encounters, he spoke confidently of his chances. 'I'm gonna rip [Paula] to shreds.' 'I'll bite [James's] teeth out,' he said one week. 'There is absolutely no way in hell I'm going home today,' he had said ahead of another boardroom. 'I'm making it to the final.' But in front of 8.4 million viewers, Clarke was dismissed. 'Ben, I think you think quite a lot of yourself,' Lord Sugar told him. 'And I think it is time, Ben, for you to leave this process: you're fired!' However, that would not be the end of his scholarship humiliation.

On the sister show *You're Fired*, he was mocked roundly about it and the programme even included a compilation of the different times he had referred to Sandhurst. So why, he was asked, did he keep referring to it? 'I didn't really have a hell of a lot on my CV,' he explained. It took him some time to live down the Sandhurst controversy and for that he had nobody to blame but himself. 'I thought I did alright,' he told the press after his exit. 'I made a bit of a c★★k out of myself and I am too young and too immature, but I learned a lot from the candidates and Sir Alan. I think I quickly learned to keep my gob shut and kept my head down for a little bit and got on a bit and I'm happy I made week nine. I did go in there all guns blazing but, to be quite honest, this is me putting my hands up. That was probably down to a lack of maturity – the fact that at twenty-two, going in there, I was very inexperienced.'

He had even faced the wrath of the officers of Sandhurst himself. A senior Sandhurst source told The *Sun* newspaper: 'Ben Clarke has let us down. Money, time and effort has been expended on him with the expectation that he would serve his country. It very much now looks like he is going to do no such thing. If he doesn't join, he has also denied the opportunity of a good education to someone else who could have been a credit to the army instead of him. He hasn't even had the good manners yet to tell us he isn't coming.'

Clarke, never short of a word or two, replied, saying he had not ruled out taking up the offer. 'It's not a case of why didn't I go, I've still got the option to go up until 2011,' he said. 'I haven't thrown the whole thing away – it's just I don't think very many people my age know what they want to do with their lives. It's a big commitment – it's a year at Sandhurst and three regular years in the army. It's an absolutely fabulous place and probably considered one of the best educations you can get.' Even in 2010, Clarke found he could not escape the Sandhurst tag. Interviewed by *Digital Spy* about his video blog commentary on *Junior Apprentice*, he was asked which of the teenage candidates had the makings of a Sandhurst scholarship. 'Tim could probably handle Sandhurst – he's a bit rough and ready, he's got fantastic taste in socks,' he said.

SCHEDULING

The Apprentice's regular scheduling is Wednesday evenings. From the start, Lord Sugar criticised the BBC for this choice of slot, as it meant it often clashed with ITV's coverage of football's UEFA Champions League matches. He felt this lost viewers. 'I can give you no better example than my own two sons. Last week they watched Chelsea-Arsenal first on Sky and then their dad afterwards on Sky Plus. That's loyalty for you.'

The most significant departure from Wednesday nights was for the finals of series five and six, which were both moved to a Sunday evening. For series five, this was to avoid a clash with ITV's coverage of an England World Cup qualifier with Andorra. 'We appreciate that many viewers will want to watch both *The Apprentice* final and the England World Cup qualifier,' said a BBC spokesperson. 'Our priority is to schedule programmes in a way that offers viewers the best experience possible.' No explicit reason was offered for the fact that the series-six final was also moved to a Sunday.

Margaret Mountford and Nick Hewer.

The channel has also been changed during the run of *The Apprentice*. Series one and two were broadcast on BBC2, then the show was moved to BBC1 from series three onwards. In his memoir Lord Sugar admits that he could not grasp the significance of this change at first, though he soon grasped what it meant in terms of both ratings and prestige. Then, of course, we had the movement of series six from the traditional springtime slot to the following autumn (See POLITICS entry). Although Lord Sugar was exasperated by the reason for this change, once it happened he felt that it proved rather successful. 'I've got a funny feeling that the BBC will be pleasantly surprised with the results of scheduling it in the autumn,' he said. 'They're going to need very, very, very big balls to move it back to spring next year.' Well, the BBC's balls must be considerable as series seven was indeed scheduled for its traditional springtime slot in 2011.

During series six, he had enjoyed the fact that the rescheduling of the run had pitched him in the same season as some heavyweight reality-television giants. For a start, it meant *The Apprentice* was running in the same time of year as Simon Cowell's *X Factor*. With characteristic self-assurance, Sugar insisted this did not trouble him one iota. 'Well, I am far superior to Cowell,' he said. 'We are completely different. Simon Cowell has got that great entertainment programme. It's an old-fashioned format that goes back many years of talent and singing competitions and it's been jazzed up nicely and it is a great show.'

He was equally as confident when it came to discussing other autumn/winter-time television shows, with which he would now face comparison. '*Strictly Come Dancing* has shocked everybody in its success,' he said. 'But we are completely different. We are a business programme which is also quite entertaining. It's like asking to compare *EastEnders* with *Match of the Day*.' If *The Apprentice* were a football programme, it would be a trophy-winning one.

SPORT RELIEF DOES THE APPRENTICE

In March 2008, BBC One broadcast a two-episode celebrity version of *The Apprentice* as part of its Sport Relief event. The men's team consisted of comedians Nick Hancock and Hardeep Singh Kohli, politician Lembit Opik, former cricketer Phil Tufnell and tabloid-journalism legend Kelvin MacKenzie. On the women's team were broadcasters Kirstie Allsopp, Lisa Snowdon and Clare Balding, together with businesswoman Jacqueline Gold.

As with the first series of *Comic Relief Does The*

COMIC RELIEF APPRENTICE NICK HANCOCK.

Apprentice, the initial boardroom meeting proved an unintentionally controversial affair. Sugar asked Kohli whether he was related to a Kohli family he had known some years ago and went on to make some light-hearted jokes about chapatis. He meant no harm by these quips and was stunned to be accused of racism by the comedian. Later in the process Kohli was again upset by a comment, this time because he felt that MacKenzie had compared him to Adolf Hitler. He walked off set. Sugar writes disparagingly of Kohli in his memoir, revealing that broadcaster Adrian Chiles had told him the comedian was a sensitive soul.

The task for each team was to fill a West End store with donated products which could be sold for charity to a specially invited, wealthy celebrity audience. In an echo of the first series of *Comic Relief Does The Apprentice* the women won comfortably, thanks in part to the presence in their number of a genuine business heavyweight, in the shape of project manager Jacqueline Gold, CEO of Ann Summers. When it came to the firing, Lord Sugar chose Hardeep Singh Kohli to face the bullet. This was not as a result of the earlier controversy, but as a result of complaints about his performance by other contestants.

As far as Lord Sugar was concerned, these celebrity spin-offs had proven to be more trouble than they were worth. 'Quite frankly, dealing with these egos in the celebrity show was starting to become a headache,' wrote Lord Sugar in his memoir, *What You See Is What You Get*. Although entertaining in themselves, the Comic Relief and Sport Relief spin-offs had indeed felt like poor relatives of the main *Apprentice* show. The desperation of some of the celebrity candidates had made the project seem more like a *Celebrity Big Brother* or *I'm A Celebrity...* style process, rather than having anything to do with the business world.

As such, they sat uncomfortably in the BBC family. Lord Sugar was not the only one to feel they were best left in the past.

SOUNDTRACK

From the opening titles of Serge Prokofiev's 'Dance of the Knights', to the moody, restrained incidental tracks, a key part of *The Apprentice*'s appeal is its brilliant soundtrack. The choice and in many cases composition of the soundtrack is down to one man – Dru Masters. Born in the 1960s, Masters has also composed music for *The Apprentice*-esque foodie series *The Restaurant* and television advertisements. He has even released a 22-track CD called *The Apprentice – Soundtrack to the BBC Series Composed by Dru Masters*. With track titles such as

CHARLIE BURDEN

Nick Hewer.

'What's Going to Happen', 'Late in the Day', 'Boardroom Loser' and 'Driving Home' it covers the different moods and moments of the series.

When Masters set about composing the soundtrack, he had a clear and grand vision of the mood he wanted to create for the series. 'We decided early on that, musically, the programme would have a slightly Sixties-Seventies caper-movie feel, sort of *The Italian Job* meets *Ocean's Eleven*,' he told The *Daily Telegraph*. It was a great decision. When compared to other reality shows, *The Apprentice* has the most admirable soundtrack. Take *The X Factor*, for instance, which regularly includes a burst of a Westlife or Leona Lewis track to soundtrack a dramatic moment (both acts earn royalties for Simon Cowell's record labels).

Interestingly, the original plan of the producers for the opening tracks had not been to use 'Dance of the Knights', but an M People-style inspirational pop song. Fortunately, Masters convinced them to go with his choice which, he explained, provides a 'suitably bombastic backdrop for Sir Alan to ham it up'. It was a wise decision. The soundtrack album was released in 2007 after sustained pressure from *Apprentice* fans. (Other official *Apprentice* merchandise to hit the shops included a book and a DVD comprising highlights of the first four series.)

Although none of them have found their way onto the shelves of music stores, there have been many musical moments on *The Apprentice*. Who will ever forget the 'Reclaim the Street' rap that Simon Ambrose performed? 'Street isn't about knowing where you're from or where you're going. Street is about where you're at. Street is about knowing yourself, knowing your style, knowing you're street – reclaim the street.'

In the aftermath of the hip-hop theme being introduced into the conversation, Margaret Mountford decided to ask the team to clue her up about a few youth-culture questions that were troubling her.

Margaret: 'What's a beatboy?'

Tre: 'Like the whole breakdancing culture that you've got going on nowadays.'

Margaret: 'What about the bump–and–grind generation?'

Ghazal: 'It's like a dance, like the tango or the twist.'

Mountford: 'Oh, right, thank you.'

The man whose voice viewers hear over the soundtrack of *The Apprentice* is narrator Mark Halliley. With a double first degree in English Literature from Cambridge, the broadcasting brainbox has worked as a presenter, director and producer on both radio and television. He also has experience as a script consultant. He has narrated *The Apprentice* since the start, it is his dulcet tones viewers hear from the start, saying: 'From across the country, sixteen tycoons of tomorrow have come to London...'

T is for...

TEAM NAMES

In episode one of each series the candidates are divided into two teams, each of which choose themselves a team name that will remain throughout the series. Their choices do not always conjure up images of business success, instead sometimes sounding more like a cheap hotel chain, a type of car or even a cinema.

    Series one: First Forte & Impact
    Series two: Invicta & Velocity
    Series three: Eclipse & Stealth
    Series four: Alpha & Renaissance

ADRIAN CHILES PRESENTED SPIN-OFF SHOW *YOU'RE FIRED*.

Series five: Empire & Ignite
Series six: Apollo & Synergy

TOYS

Never work with children or animals, goes the well-known quote from American comedian W.C. Fields. Some *Apprentice* candidates would argue that it is not just children one should never work with, but toys as well. Whenever toys have been involved in *Apprentice* tasks they have managed to send candidates into appalling flaps. The toy traumas started in the second week of the first ever series. By placing this task so early in the series, when all but one of the series candidates are still in the process, it layered extra difficulty onto the creative process as multiple contrasting opinions and ideas were passionately aired.

With so many competing ideas and clashing egos, the territory of this task was fertile for disaster. There was a danger that someone would throw the toys out of the pram before a final toy product was even agreed upon. As it turned out, it was the women's team, First Forte, who came unstuck in this episode – and in some style. In truth, they had been up against it from the start, when the men's team omitted to inform them that the call had come through from *Apprentice* headquarters, meaning the ladies had less time to prepare for the task. Once the challenge actually got underway, it was one of those occasions when there was no doubt whatsoever as to who was responsible for the failure of the task – the terrifyingly tenacious team leader Lindsay.

Her idea for a new toy was a peculiar product called 'Secret Signals' – cards with which children could learn about semaphore signals. It seemed a product that was unlikely to succeed among 21st-century kids. Her team-mates did not like the idea and nor did a 'focus group' of children, but she remained impervious to the growing consensus. Another idea for a toy robot was mooted, but it was not to get the green light. In one of the most audacious decisions ever made in *Apprentice* history, she stubbornly decided to stick with her idea. 'I, as project manager, want to take a risk,' she said to widespread horror.

Meanwhile, the men's team approached matters more sensibly. They remained open to feedback and developed an electronic trading-game product that was far more viable than Lindsay's 'Secret Signal' cards. The executives of top toy manufacturer Vivid listened patiently to pitches for each of the teams' products and declared that the Impact one was the clear winner. Apart from Lindsay, few were at all surprised by this. Lord Sugar strongly agreed with the executives and, in one of the easiest *Apprentice* boardroom decisions he has ever made, he told Lindsay: 'You're fired!' This task would have been a perfect one for series-six candidate Sandeesh Samra, who started her professional life as a sales assistant at Toys 'R' Us. For Lindsay, it was a nightmare, thanks to her stubborn stance.

Two weeks deeper into the series and toys were once more firmly on the agenda. Personal friend of Lord Sugar, Mohammed Al Fayed, allowed *The Apprentice* to host a sales-led task in the Harrods toy department. It was a task with plenty of adrenalin and a twist in its tail. Tim's First Forte team showed greater imagination in the opening stages, employing the services of a face painter and toy demonstrator. This guaranteed their stand plenty of attention, which their opponents, Impact, could only look at with envy and despair.

However, Saira sold her socks off and Paul gamely donned a bear outfit to drum up attention. With her last sale of the day, Saira won the task for Impact. This was the first episode in which nobody was technically fired. Adele could see that Lord Sugar was growing increasingly critical of her and chose to resign from proceedings before it even came to the final boardroom showdown. Her parting words were that she was an 'easy target' who other contestants felt threatened by. Lord Sugar confirmed that she would have been fired had she not resigned (though that could only have happened if Tim had brought her into the boardroom).

In week nine of series two, Lord Sugar tasked the teams to each choose a nation to represent in the form of a selling task. Tre's Eclipse team decided to choose Swedish products, including wheat-filled, microwaveable soft toys. Lord Sugar told Tre he had 'messed up big time', but he granted him a reprieve when it came to the all-important dismissal. Instead, he fired Jadine. 'I accept that you are a go-getter or a fighter,' he told her. 'But I don't think you're a finished product for me. Jadine, you're fired!'

The moral of many of these toy stories of *The Apprentice* is that it is not a product to be treated as kids' play. Other playthings that have featured during tasks include the infra-red air guitar that Ignite tried to sell during the series-five teleshopping week, only to lose the task. Then there was the toy that the teams were challenged to create in the first instalment of COMIC RELIEF DOES THE APPRENTICE (see entry).

TWITTER

Lord Sugar is one of the most followed celebrities on the Twitter social-networking website. He has had some entertaining spats on the website, including with

APPRENTICE CONTESTANT KATIE HOPKINS.

controversial *Daily Mail* columnist Jan Moir after she had criticised the celebrities who used Twitter to offer condolences to Amanda Holden when she lost her baby. He wrote: 'Mega bitch Jan Moir in Daily Liar says extending condolences is showing off. Fact: If something bad happens to her there will be silence.'

He has also pursued an ongoing – mostly tongue-in-cheek – row with celebrity journalist and former *Comic Relief Does The Apprentice* contestant Piers Morgan, who he has described as 'monkey', a 'pathetic grovler' [sic], a 'saddo' and a 'DBT – a double-barrel tosser'. Morgan replied in kind, as a highly-entertaining war of words developed between them. He regularly corrected Lord Sugar's spelling mistakes and described *The Apprentice* boss as a 'disingenuous old growler' who had 'anger-management issues'.

A celebrity who has used Twitter to be more praising of Sugar is pop singer Lily Allen. 'Could Alan Sugar use a few more metaphors in his opener? Diamonds, coal, extreme pressure! LOL,' she wrote in March 2009. 'I'm harder to play than a Stradivarius, you're as easy to play as the bongo drums. Genius. I know the words to 'Candle in the Wind', that don't make me Elton John!'

Lord Sugar has used his Twitter account to regularly plug his memoir, *What You See Is What You Get*. He delights in re-tweeting messages sent to him from readers who had enjoyed the book. In November 2010, he was blasted when he broke a two-minute Twitter silence he had suggested on Armistice Day, by sending out a Tweet plugging his book during the supposed silence. He blamed the mistake on 'a technical glitch'. He also announces details of forthcoming *Apprentice* instalments on Twitter. In February 2011, he revealed the change that will be made to the format of the show for its seventh series. He wrote that the 'next series of apprentice in May will end with the winner starting a new business with me on a 50/50 basis where I inject £250k'.

Here are the Twitter usernames for key *Apprentice* figures.

Lord Sugar: @Lord_Sugar

Donald Trump: @realDonaldTrump

Dara Ó Briain: @daraobriain

If you want to read the banter between Lord Sugar and other celebrities he regularly chats and spars with on Twitter, follow:

Piers Morgan: @PiersMorgan

Duncan Bannatyne: @DuncanBannatyne

Peter Jones: @DragonJones

U is for...

UNDERWEAR

In the second episode of series four, the teams were charged with a laundry task. Each were given the use of an industrial laundry for a night, and sent out to drum up trade in order to make use of it. In the boardroom, one of the teams tried to justify its high prices by explaining that a customer-care phone line was included in the price. Sugar wondered aloud what sort of calls such a phone line would take: 'Can you tell me how my Calvin Klein's are getting on, please?'

This was not the only time that Sugar has turned a boardroom conversation round to the matter of

KATE WALSH AND PHILIP TAYLOR.

underwear. 'You are not here to enhance some sort of media career,' he once warned the contestants. 'So if any of you gentlemen are thinking of prancing around in your Calvin Kleins, showing off your three-piece-suite bulge you can forget about it.' It was a female contestant who did the most eye-catching underwear shoot. In January 2011, 25-year-old stunner Joanna Riley did a lingerie shoot for lad's magazine *Zoo*. 'I just wanted to bring the fun side of me out because in *The Apprentice*, I was very professional and business-like,' she said. 'I wanted to prove you can still be sexy in business as well and hopefully I've done that.' She certainly had.

However, *The Apprentice* underwear moment that will not be forgotten in a hurry was that of Pantsman. The advertising round in *The Apprentice,* in which the candidates are asked to create campaigns for a product, often produces memorably zany concepts. The Pantsman character was such an idea, dreamed up by team Ignite. The character, to promote a breakfast cereal called Wake-Up Call, was the brainchild of Durham estate agent Philip Taylor. 'Sometimes you have to think outside the box if you want to push a few boundaries,' he said. Well, he certainly lived true to that principle with Pantsman.

During the advert, Taylor sang the catchy song that began: 'At the start of the day, everybody knows,

without your wake-up call you put your pants over your clothes.' Meanwhile, Noorul Choudhury danced around the kitchen, wearing the Pantsman costume. Fortunately, Choudhury was keen to get involved in the spirit of things. 'I really enjoyed it actually and I think you should always do what your team manager asks, otherwise you come across as bitter and twisted,' he said. (He later admitted to the media that he had a fling with a grandmother, so he is clearly willing to give anything a go.)

Lord Sugar was not convinced by the overall concept, to put it politely. 'Total garbage, absolute garbage,' he said. Luckily for Taylor, he avoided the chop that week. Meanwhile, the Pantsman character had captured the imagination of the viewing public. One online shop created Pantsman merchandise including T-shirts and mugs. The memory of that episode lingers. When Taylor ran the 2009 Great North Run, he did so dressed as Pantsman. He has since attempted to shake-off the legacy. 'I'm still infamous for the "Pantsman" episode and the sooner I can get away from that the better,' said Taylor.

V is for...

VIEWING FIGURES

Series one drew an average audience of 2.5 million and an 11 per cent share of the available audience. Figures peaked at 3.8 million for the final. Series-two figures were up, averaging at 4.4 million (a 19 per cent share), peaking at 6.0 million and 27 per cent for the final show. The final beat the UEFA Cup Final figures on ITV, even though British side Middlesbrough were competing. This was a sweet victory for Sugar, who had worried about the effect going head to head with European football would have on *Apprentice* ratings.

Series three suffered at times from the clashes with popular Channel 4 reality series *Big Brother*. But *The*

Apprentice final drew 6.8 million for its final, 27.4 per cent of viewers. In series four, it set a new record when it grabbed a whopping 6.4 million viewers for its opening episode. It also broke past records in the final, which was watched by 8.9 million viewers. This was 36 per cent of the viewing public. Some five million stayed tuned for the *You're Hired* show that followed. The opener of series five drew 8.11 million viewers and series six peaked at 8.2 million.

Series five started on a high when the opening episode was watched by an impressive 8.1 million viewers. It continued to soar from there and captured over 10 million people for its grand finale. By the time series six came along, the figures were rising and rising. Even early episodes in the season drew more than 7 million viewers and by the time it came to the final 8.3 million viewers were watching. In between, it had been hit by the interest in ITV's *I'm A Celebrity...* programme, but it had beaten television coverage of England's friendly match with France in November.

As for the *Junior Apprentice*, it suffered initially by the fact it went head to head with the final series of Channel 4's *Big Brother*. While 4.2 million watched the *Junior Apprentice*, up to 5.9 million were watching the launch of *Big Brother*. However, the show improved from there, and had reached over 5 million viewers by episode three.

W is for...

WEAKEST LINK

In 2008, there was a special *Apprentice*-themed edition of the popular BBC quiz, *The Weakest Link*, featuring candidates from all the series to date. Here, at last, the candidates who had been fired by Lord Sugar after battling and bitching with one another had a chance to get even with one another. 'This will be the ultimate *Weakest Link* – nine people with huge egos who have plenty of scores to settle,' said an insider in the run-up to the show.

Indeed, in this show it would be the contestants who did the firing, by voting one another off at the end of

JENNY CELERIER APPEARED ON *THE WEAKEST LINK*.

each round. It began with a special *Apprentice*-flavoured voiceover introduction. 'From across the country, nine *Apprentice* candidates have come to London. They are here to compete for a huge cash prize for the charity of their choice.' The quiz had attracted some of the show's most outrageous and controversial characters including Katie Hopkins, Syed Ahmed and Tre Azam. Also lining up were Nicholas De Lacy-Brown and Kristina Grimes. Completing the panel to be quizzed by Anne Robinson were Jenny Celerier, Kevin Shaw, James Max and Ian Stringer.

It proved to be a feisty experience. When Robinson challenged Hopkins about her tendency to date married men, Hopkins gave as good as she got. 'I think in this world, Anne, we need to learn to share,' she said. She then told the host that her husband had run off with another woman. 'Did that surprise you?' asked Anne. The host then turned to Hopkins' old nemesis Grimes and asked her to sum up Hopkins. 'I think she's a liar, a cheat, a fake,' said Grimes. 'I object to the fact she is compared to horses because I like horses.'

The final two contestants were Jo Cameron and Kristina Grimes, who went head to head in the five-question knockout final round. It proved an embarrassing experience as they fluffed question after question. Grimes even failed to name the current Chancellor of the

Exchequer. 'It's going very well,' said Robinson after seven questions. 'Nobody has answered a single question correctly so far.' Then, Cameron finally answered a question correctly and when Grimes fluffed her next one, that sealed the win for Cameron.

It was appropriate for *The Apprentice* and *The Weakest Link* shows to combine. After all, Anne Robinson is the television personality who made blunt speaking to members of the public so fashionable. Her pithy put-downs on the quiz show came long before the likes of Sugar and Cowell added their own straight-talking voices to the airwaves. It is a pity Lord Sugar himself was not among the contestants on *The Weakest Link*. A head-to-head between him and Robinson would make for gripping, explosive small-screen entertainment.

What a battle it would be. Who would emerge on top? Would it be a case of: 'You are the weakest link, goodbye,' or: 'You're fired'?

WINNERS

Here are the lucky winners of the first six series.

Series one: Tim Campbell

A Psychology graduate from Middlesex University, he worked in the strategic and marketing department of

Tim Campbell.

London Underground before he applied to *The Apprentice*. He proved a popular and able candidate from the start, taking on the team-leader mantle in weeks one and four. He remained calm and professional, even as some of the other candidates fought and backstabbed. 'I was constantly aware it was a job interview, not *Big Brother*,' he said. 'The criticism thrown at me is that I kind of disappear. But a big part of business is to observe.' The only flashpoint he was involved in came when he wished a recently fired candidate good luck. 'You're going to fucking need good luck,' she replied.

However, after an entertaining final that pitched Campbell against Saira Khan, he was crowned the first apprentice, despite making less money than his rival contestant. Explaining his decision, Lord Sugar said: 'It was a tough decision, but Tim is a great fella and I think I've chosen the best of the bunch. I've found my real apprentice.' He appointed Campbell the first Project Director of the Health & Beauty division of Amstrad PLC. One of his first tasks was to market an anti-wrinkle cream.

He left Amstrad two years later, with a ringing recommendation from Lord Sugar. 'He has been a great asset to the company and I wish him the best of luck for the future. He was the right choice and I will be there to offer any help and guidance should he need it.'

SERIES-TWO WINNER MICHELLE DEWBERRY.

Campbell set-up the Bright Ideas Trust, which offered a range of support to budding entrepreneurs between the ages of 16 and 30. He has also served as Social Enterprise Ambassador for the Government.

He enjoyed his *Apprentice* experience, more because of, rather than inspite of, the rough-and-tumble nature of the contest. 'I come from a world where everything is politically correct,' he said. 'Being in a situation where things are actually expressed was quite refreshing.' However, he has avoided the temptation to leap into the world of celebrity, as a result of his *Apprentice*-found fame. '*The Apprentice* gave me the opportunity to get a job and I'm glad I didn't sell my soul to the celebrity world,' he said. 'The problem with the world of celebrity is it can be incredibly fickle.'

Series two: Michelle Dewberry

The winner of the second series of *The Apprentice* says her work ethic and ambition was instilled in her by her father. The glamorous, impressive lady from Hull had left school with just two GCSEs and a year later she lost her sister, after she fell to her death from an eighth-floor window. This spurred Dewberry to work harder and by the time she was 24 she ran her own telecoms business. Throughout the series she performed well.

She beat Ruth Badger in the final, which saw the pair

organise rival parties on Tower Bridge. Dewberry's James Bond evening outshone her rival's murder-mystery bash. Despite that, it proved a difficult choice for Lord Sugar when it came to picking the winner. 'It was very, very tough,' he said. 'Last year was much easier, there was no contest.' Dewberry admitted she was surprised she won, as she said she is not an 'overly confident' person. Her success on the show had echoes of that enjoyed by Tim Campbell. 'It shows you don't need to be loud and cocky and "bolshie" – just work as hard as you can and hopefully you will get on in life,' she said. Many felt that her gentle demeanour concealed steeliness within and she earned the nickname 'Silent Assassin'.

However, as with other *Apprentice* candidates down the years, she feels that the editing of the programme slanted perceptions of her in a particular direction. 'They underplayed me on screen all the way through so it would be a real shock when I made it into a final,' she said. 'I'm not as dull and quiet as I've been edited to seem.' There could be little glossing over the heartache and disappointments she endured in the aftermath of the show. She had a fling with fellow candidate Syed Ahmed and became pregnant by him. She then tragically lost the baby after a miscarriage in August 2006. In the wake of that tragedy the couple split.

Simon Ambrose

She left her job at Amstrad within months of her victory and there is surely significance that she was the only *Apprentice* winner not featured in the photo-section, nor the text, of Lord Sugar's memoir, *What You See Is What You Get*. She has popped up in the media on occasion, including a stint doing weather reports on the late, great ITV breakfast show GMTV. She now runs an online business-advice surgery.

Series three: Simon Ambrose

Former Westminster schoolboy and Cambridge graduate Simon Ambrose described himself as social, dynamic and disorganised. During a testing childhood in a broken home he idolised Lord Sugar, the man who would later employ him. He had worked for the investment bank Credit Suisse prior to applying to the third series of *The Apprentice*.

He described his time on the show as a 'crazy, intense experience'. The most memorable moment of his *Apprentice* journey came in the teleshopping task when he demonstrated how to assemble a trampoline. As he twisted one of the legs into the base the scene became uncomfortably phallic. Adrian Chiles, presenter of spin-off show *You're Fired* was moved to describe this as the 'greatest piece of TV ever'. Ambrose also made for an unlikely but semi-convincing rapper

CLAIRE YOUNG WAS
BEATEN BY LEE MCQUEEN
IN SERIES FOUR.

when he performed the 'Reclaim the Streets' song during a task to promote trainers.

His victory over single mother Kristina Grimes in the final proved controversial. 'Bloody old fool that I am, I'm going to take that risk, you're hired,' Lord Sugar told him in a less-than-ringing endorsement. Many felt that Grimes had outperformed Ambrose throughout the process. Even the runner-up herself was open about her feelings. 'I felt I'd out-performed Simon – he's a lovely chap but I still think I should have won,' she said.

Ambrose joined Amsprop in 2007 and set to work developing a £70 million hotel and golf complex near Stansted Airport in Essex. After three years he left to start his own property development firm. Lord Sugar said: 'Having learned the ropes at Amsprop, Simon is leaving to pursue his own personal projects and we wish him the best of luck for the future.'

Series four: Lee McQueen

A gravelly-voiced, six-foot two milkman's son, Lee McQueen was described well by The *Daily Telegraph* as 'the quintessential rough diamond-cum-unreconstructed Neanderthal – the barrow boy's barrow boy'. He made for an unlikely winner. During the semi-final interview round he was forced to admit that he had lied in his CV. However, he had improved the longer the series went on and triumphantly beat Claire Young in the final.

McQueen was television gold. He had made *Apprentice* viewers laugh from the start with his tendency to refer to himself in the third person: 'I'm concerned – Lee McQueen is concerned.' While team leader during the task in Marrakech, he performed an amusing impersonation of an alarm clock and also a rendition of a 'reverse pterodactyl'. The laughs continued to the end. When Young told him during the final that she felt sick, he replied: 'I feel sick too. Shall we just be sick together?'

His victory was indeed something of a surprise, not least because he had been caught lying in his CV during the interview round. McQueen had claimed to have spent two years at college but had in truth spent only four months there. He admitted it was a 'massive mistake' and that he was 'extremely disappointed' with himself. He explained that he felt uncomfortable about his modest educational qualifications.

McQueen's *Apprentice* time will be most remembered for his endlessly repeated catchphrase: 'That's what I'm talking about.' In one episode he said it once every six minutes and it quickly became a favourite term of reference among *Apprentice* viewers. The catchphrase followed McQueen even after the series had ended. He remembered with horror the time Lord Sugar and he were going to a meeting in Canary Wharf. Passers-by kept shouting the phrase at McQueen, who found the experience uncomfortable.

In the wake of the series, McQueen was given a job in Sugar's Amscreen company. He struck a lucrative five-year deal with BP that saw digital advertising screens installed on BP forecourts across the country. He also sealed a great deal with HMV. These were great moments for him after a dodgy start to his Amscreen career. He had to phone in sick on his very first day, because he was struggling with a 'flu-like virus'. This naturally hit the headlines, but a spokesman for Lord Sugar was keen to emphasise that there was no problem. 'He's certainly not furious,' said the spokesman. 'People get ill and he understands that.'

McQueen left Sugar's employ in 2010 to take up a career in public speaking. It was said to be a 'cordial' departure. Lord Sugar commented: 'Lee has made an important contribution to Amscreen and we wish him the best.' Final word on McQueen goes to the woman he beat in final, Claire Young. 'I'd shag him,' she said. An honest and unflinching comment. In 2009 McQueen had faced legal action from Amscreen colleague Hanna Sebright, who claimed he had made sexist remarks in front of her. Sebright later dropped her case.

Series five: Yasmina Siadatan

The former restaurateur was named the 'Alpha female' when she was crowned the winner of *The Apprentice*. She had studied Economic History at the London School of Economics and Political Science prior to applying to the show. Most viewers had expected her rival Kate Walsh to win the final, but Lord Sugar went with his 'gut instinct' and told Siadatan: 'You're hired,' after a final task in which the candidates had to create a new box of chocolates.

She came close to disaster twice in the series. The first was during the cosmetics task, when her team failed to spot a 400 per cent price difference between cedarwood and sandalwood. 'I thought I was going to get fired,' she said. 'It was horrendous. Literally like your heart dropping out of the bottom of your pants.' The second time was during the interviews round when Claude Littner gave her a savage grilling, which in her own words 'turned into a raw interrogation about my business accounts'.

Her confusion over figures and palpable discomfort as Littner revealed he had acquired her accounts from Companies House were toe curling. She looked anything but a winner at this stage, but it was her that Lord Sugar chose to hire come the final reckoning. 'I can't believe it, I am in shock,' she said in the aftermath of the show. 'All those months ago you first apply to try to get on, and here I am. It's amazing.' It was a wonderful vote of confidence for the woman who said she was inspired by her 'wheeler dealer' father, who reminded her of Lord Sugar.

On winning the show, she was put to work at Amscreen Health Care, where she would sell digital signage to the National Health Service. 'I've been adaptable my whole life, so I relish the opportunity to work in a digital signage company now,' she said. Soon after starting work she fell for one of her colleagues, Andrew Hepburn. Soon after he left Amscreen, Siadatan fell pregnant by him and the couple moved in together. 'Life is brilliant at the moment,' she said. 'We're really enjoying everything that comes with it.'

Series six: Stella English

Her victory in *The Apprentice* was a true 'against the odds' story, for Stella English grew up on one of Britain's most notorious council estates. She moved between care homes and relatives and later drank in a pub notorious for the violent criminals who frequented it. She was determined to rise above this and completed a one-year business course before becoming a business manager with top firms such as Merrill Lynch.

The mother-of-two developed a reputation as an 'ice maiden' during the tasks. She often clashed with her fellow candidates, including Stuart Baggs. Although she could sometimes come across as wooden, she livened up

STELLA ENGLISH AND CHRIS BATES.

the longer the series went on. When she guided a tour bus of visitors around east London, she gamely sang 'Knees Up Mother Brown' to add to the cockney atmosphere. Her rival Laura Moore stepped in to dispel suggestions that Stella was a less than warm character. She said: 'Stella's not cold. She comes from a very corporate background in banking where only the toughest survive, so she does have that side to her. But she's a lot softer in person and I got on with her really well.'

Stella's rival in the final was Chris Bates, an investment banker from Surrey who prided himself on being one of Britain's foremost scholars of theology. The pair were handed the task of creating and marketing a new alcoholic drink. She created 'a bourbon blend for the new generation' called Urbon. Her performance during this task (and throughout the series in general) was enough to land her those golden words: 'You're hired.'

Lord Sugar is a fitting boss for English, who once said of herself: 'Like a dog with a bone, I can't let go. If I want something, I get it.' That tenacity was key to winning the approval of Lord Sugar, who had originally feared that she might be too corporate to thrive in any of his companies. Her advice for aspiring business people is to take responsibility for their own lives. 'I've spent a long time blaming other people, but the time my life really turned around for the best was when I stopped doing that.'

CONTESTANT AND STELLA RIVAL LAURA MOORE.

X is for...

XENOPHOBIA

In series six, Lord Sugar sent the hopefuls to Hamburg in Germany to try and sell new flavours of crisps to local businesses. During the task, former Royal Marines sniper Christopher Farrell said: 'I hate the Germans,' and his three team-mates burst out laughing. However, when word reached Germany about this sentiment, they were not amused. 'We all know about the history – people suffered on both sides,' Hamburg resident Peter Kuhn said. 'You hope that people have moved on. The sad thing is, you would expect modern Brits to be more grown-up but, sadly, some seem to be pretty xenophobic.'

A more light-hearted moment on the show had been when Stuart Baggs had attempted to speak German to the locals. While he deserves credit for trying, his attempts at German occasionally fell comically flat. He called himself 'Herr Baggs' when he phoned companies to make appointments. When he sat down alongside fellow contestant Laura to pitch to some Germans, he said: 'Good morning, I'm Stuart and this is my male colleague, Laura. We are pleased and here to be.'

As Lord Sugar later pondered: 'Harebrained or Herr Baggs?' However, he was to face controversy himself as a result of a light-hearted quip he made during a conversation with Baggs. During a boardroom show-down, Lord Sugar asked Baggs why he should not fire him. Baggs said: 'If you give me one hundred grand a year, I will deliver to you ten times that and if I don't – take it all back. A money-back guarantee, I'm that confident.' Lord Sugar replied: 'I had an offer like that from Nigeria once and funnily enough it didn't transpire.'

His joke seemed to be in reference to the notorious email scams, in which emails are sent asking people for money, under titles such as 'Confidential Business Proposal'. However, the Nigerian High Commissioner, His Excellency Dr Dalhatu Sarki Tafida, did not see the funny side. 'Lord Sugar's remark on Nigeria is preposterous and spurious for a number

CONTESTANT YASMINA SIADATAN.

of reasons,' he said. 'It was an unprovoked, damaging remark on a sovereign and independent state of over one hundred and fifty million people, based on his alleged sordid and isolated deal with a Nigerian individual. It is indeed demeaning and unfortunate.'

It was surprising that the often cautious and politically correct BBC had allowed such a potentially contentious joke to make the final cut of the programme. A spokesman for the corporation said: 'It is clear Lord Sugar was just making a reference to a perception about email scams. I think that was what the remark was about and a person has chosen to make a comment on it. It is clear what he was referring to and I don't think it can be seen as a comment against the whole Nigerian nation.'

In April 2009, the media wondered whether there had been a hint of racism at work when Yasmina Siadatan had asked white team-mate Philip Taylor to replace Asian Noorul Choudhury in a commercial for their task product because she favoured a mix of ethnic backgrounds. However, Majid Nagra insisted there was nothing sinister at play. Nagra told the BBC: 'It was a small thing that was blown way out of proportion. I think from a business point of view you've got to cater for everything, whether it be a white man, a green man, a yellow man, a purple man, it doesn't really matter.' He added: 'In the house everybody got on with everybody, there was no such thing as race, there was no such thing as that, it never even materialised.'

There have been other allegations of politically incorrect 'phobias' being at work during the series. It was suggested that gay candidate Howard Ebison was offended when team-mate Mona Lewis turned down his idea to introduce a gay theme to a task involving the rebranding of Margate as a holiday resort. 'Howard did very well to keep his cool as he was extremely offended,' said an unnamed source. 'He had to put up with a certain amount of homophobic abuse when he was growing up, so this really upset him.' Lewis denied such a problem had arisen. Ebison, too, insisted that there had been no such controversy. 'I've not been upset or experienced any homophobic remarks at all on the show,' he said. 'I have no issues with any candidate.'

Then came the attack Sugar faced for a remark he made to a candidate who suffered from arthritis. When he fired former footballer and arthritis sufferer Rocky Andrews, he told him: 'Your career at Middlesbrough was halted. You got taken off the pitch in a stretcher. This time you're off the pitch in a black cab. Rocky, you're fired.' Jane Tadman, from the Arthritis Research Campaign, was not amused. 'We are always trying to move away from negative images of arthritis,' Tadman told the *Daily Star Sunday*. 'I think a lot of people think arthritis only affects older people but it can affect anyone – even babies. Sir Alan's comments are pretty negative and not welcome.'

An accusation that has been made against Lord Sugar is that he harbours sexist opinions about women's roles in the workplace. He strongly denies the charge. 'I have great sympathy for women,' he said. 'I think some of the employment laws are counter-productive. They prevent employers asking questions, which ninety-nine per cent of the women would be happy to answer...Where they live, whether they have children, have they made provision to have their children looked after. It gets blown out of proportion by the media.'

Y is for...

YOU'RE FIRED

The Apprentice's catchphrase is uttered by Lord Sugar at the end of each episode (apart from the final, in which he instead utters 'You're hired'). 'Personally, I'd have liked the flexibility to be able to vary it, to say, "you're sacked" or "get out" or possibly even "clear off",' said Lord Sugar. 'But they tell me "you're fired" is great TV.' Not that he has gone all soft on us, as he showed when he went to explain: 'On the other hand, there are certain types of people I have no trouble firing: the lazy, the incompetent, the disloyal.'

Throughout the first six series of *The Apprentice*, he

You're Fired host Dara Ó Briain.

inserted memorable put-downs into the firing process. During series three, he said to Rory Laing: 'I was told that you... [have] been bankrupt twice. Well, here's the hat-trick... Rory, you're fired!' In series four he told Nicholas de Lacy-Brown: 'You were devastated when you got a B in your GCSE French. You're going to be even more devastated now, because you've got a big F. You're fired!' In series six to Stuart Baggs: 'My advisers... said to me that you're full of shit! You're fired.'

Here are the phrases used to dismiss candidates in *Apprentice* shows from other countries:

Brazil: *Voc' est demitido.*

Denmark: *Du er fyret.*

Germany: *Sie haben frei.* (You are excused.)

India: In the Indian version the fired candidate is handed an air ticket.

Indonesia: *Anda saya pecat!* (I fire you.)

Norway: *Du har sparken.*

Russia: Вы уволены

Switzerland: *Sie sind raus!* (You are out.)

Turkey: *Seninle çalışmak istemiyorum!* (I do not want to work with you.)

You're Fired is also the name of the sister show to *The Apprentice*. The 30-minute spin-off was launched to accompany the second series in 2006 and was first shown on BBC Three. Presented by Adrian Chiles, it went out immediately after the main show finished. It featured humorous discussion of the latest episode, and an interview with the fired candidate. Studio guests discuss the episode and the progress of the series in general. The air of irreverence made it compulsive viewing from the off. It proved such a successful and popular show that it was moved to BBC 2 in 2007. In 2010, comedian Dara Ó Briain replaced Chiles as the host. Controller of BBC 2, Janice Hadlow, said: 'I'm thrilled to have Dara on board. His unique style of quick-witted banter is ideally suited to the job of probing the latest casualty of Lord Sugar's infamous firing finger.'

It features many running features including 'Quote of the Week' and 'The One That Got Away'. At the end of each episode, the host asks the studio audience whether they agree that the correct candidate was fired. They vote by holding up either a green or red card, with the latter indicating they disagreed with the decision. Traditionally, the host then presents the fired candidate with a parting gift, usually in homage to a humorous or embarrassing moment they endured during the series. At the end of the show, the fired candidate is shown a compilation of their 'best bits', in a direct echo of the eviction shows of former Channel 4 reality series *Big Brother*. The final feature of each

MICHELLE DEWBERRY.

episode is a brief trail of the next week's episode of the main *Apprentice* show.

Following the final of each *Apprentice* series, the spin-off show is called *You're Hired*. It's a longer affair, lasting at least an hour, where Lord Sugar joins the panel and looks back over the entire series. Another spin-off from *The Apprentice* is the programme *Why I Fired Them*, in which Lord Sugar looks back on the unsuccessful candidates in the series. Reliving their most terrible decisions, Lord Sugar reveals how, each week, he decided who would hear his famous phrase: 'You're fired.'

YOU'RE HIRED

It is the climax of the series, when Lord Sugar finally chooses who will be the winner and the recipient of the six-figure job in one of his companies. With just two candidates left in the boardroom, he invites them to make a final case for themselves. He then weighs up his options agonisingly, as the tension builds. Finally, he lifts his famous finger, points it at his chosen winner and tells them: 'You're hired.'

However, all is not quite as it seems to the viewer.

The programme makers, in fact, film two separate outcomes, each one casting one of the candidates as the winner. Sugar then spends several months (or weeks depending on the series) deciding which of the two to hire. He tells the candidates which of them has won, shortly before the final is aired. His announcement often takes place over a private lunch or dinner with the finalists. Until this stage he is the only person who knows his decision. He shares it with the production team at the same time as he tells the candidates. The correct candidate's 'You're hired' moment is then broadcast, while the other version is left on the cutting-room floor. If you have ever wondered why the winning candidate sometimes looks less than exhilarated when they are told: 'You're hired,' this is why.

The period between the filming of the final programme and its editing has been anywhere between several weeks and several months. In the case of series six, it was nearly a year due to a delay in the broadcasting. During the intermediary period, both finalists are found temporary work in one of Lord Sugar's companies. The official reason for this is that, as they are unable to seek employment until after the transmission, they are given these jobs out of fairness. Sceptics suggest that these temporary roles are also given to them so Lord Sugar can continue to judge their effectiveness. Or, to put it another way, the two finalists are still on trial long after the final episode is filmed.

Interestingly, Lord Sugar admits in his memoir that 'there's a certain resentment from some of the staff' at his companies when the winner officially joins their ranks. Their feelings are understandable. For 12 weeks they will have seen the candidate on television, including many cock-ups. So when the winner arrives, with a widely publicised six-figure salary, such feelings are inevitable. It's all part of the tough process that is *The Apprentice* but Lord Sugar does his best to keep the morale of everybody in his companies high as the new faces settle in.

Z is for...

ZOO

In week four of series three, the candidates were charged with the task of producing and selling confectionary that they could sell to children at London Zoo. With the rival teams desperate for victory, somewhat underhand tactics were employed. Christina swept up to families and placed her team's lollipops directly into the hands of their children. With the kids excited by this development, she would turn to the parents and ask for payment. As for Tre Azam, he chose to specifically target fat people. It was all very *Apprentice* behaviour.

Lord Sugar is not a fan of all animals. 'I don't want the RSPCA, doggie and cat lovers to start jumping, but I don't like dogs and cats,' he said. 'End of story.'

ACKNOWLEDGEMENTS

Thanks to all who have offered help, support and advice on this and my other *Apprentice*-related books. Particular thanks on that note to Lucian Randall, Stuart Robertson, Rosie Virgo and John Blake. Thanks also to all involved with *The Apprentice*, for so many hours of entertaining, inspiring and amusing television.

If the author were to pick a favourite episode, it would undoubtedly be episode two of series two, when Invicta and Velocity pitched rival calendars to retailers. ...dropping, mesmerising television.

...avourite candidate? That's a tough one. Maybe ...mpbell? No, Ruth Badger. Or, hang on, what ...Syed Ahmed or Yasmina Siadatan? Then there's ...ayou. Either him or Stuart Baggs (the brand). I ...iked Alex Epstein, actually...

BIBLIOGRAPHY

Alan Sugar: The Amstrad Story – David Thomas
(Pan Books 1991)

Lord Sugar: The Man Who Revolutionised British Business
– Charlie Burden (John Blake 2010)

Sir Alan Sugar: The Biography – Charlie Burden
(John Blake 2009)

What You See Is What You Get – Alan Sugar
(Macmillan 2010)